School Recess
and Playground Behavior

SUNY Series, Children's Play in Society

Anthony D. Pellegrini, Editor

School Recess
and Playground Behavior

Educational and
Developmental Roles

Anthony D. Pellegrini

State University of New York Press

Published by
State University of New York Press, Albany

© 1995 State University of New York

For information, address State University of New York Press,
State University Plaza, Albany, N.Y. 12246

Production by M. R. Mulholland
Marketing by Bernadette La Manna

Library of Congress Cataloging-in-Publication Data

Pellegrini, Anthony D.
    School recess and playground behavior : educational and
developmental roles / Anthony D. Pellegrini.
        p.   cm. — (SUNY series, children's play in society)
    Includes bibliographical references (p.   ) and index.
    ISBN 0-7914-2183-X. — ISBN 0-7914-2184-8 (pbk.)
    1. Recesses. 2. Play—United States. 3. Child development.
4. Educational surveys—United States. I. Title. II. Series.
LB3033.P45 1995
371.2′424—dc20   93-50547
                                                              CIP

10 9 8 7 6 5 4 3 2 1

To P., with much thanks.

"You say you don't see much in it all; nothing but a struggling mass of boys, and a leather ball, which seems to excite them to a great fury, as a red rag does a bull. My dear sir, a battle would look much the same to you, except that the boys would be men, and the balls iron; but a battle would be worth your looking at for all that, and so is a football match. You can't be expected to appreciate the delicate strokes of play, the turns by which a game is lost and won, - it takes an old player to do that, but the broad philosophy of football you can understand if you will. Come along with me a little nearer, and let us consider it altogether." (p. 99)

—T. Hughes (1895). *Tom Brown's School Days*.
Cambridge: The Riverside Press.

Contents

Acknowledgments

This volume reflects years of work on a rather specific topic. Thus, I have a rather long list of acknowledgments. My initial work on children's playground behavior was funded by a grant from the Sarah Moss Foundation at the University of Georgia. This fellowship allowed my family and I to spend three months in Sheffield where the seeds of my interest in the topic were planted. Seven years later we were back in Sheffield for a longer stay, supported by a Senior International Fellowship from the National Institutes of Health. Over the years the Sheffield connection has been vital to my work. The intellectual and social support of the Department of Psychology there has made my stays at Sheffield stimulating and enjoyable. Specifically, the department heads Chris Spencer and Kevin Connolly were most cordial and supportive. Most importantly, Peter K. Smith served as my mentor in the study of children's play, ethological methods, and asking provocative questions.

Another mentor is Brian Sutton-Smith. Over the years Brian has been a model scholar, asking the interesting and novel questions, insisting that we try to see things as children do.

Other sources of support must be acknowledged, for without them this work certainly would not have been undertaken. The Harry Frank Guggenheim Foundation provided support for my work with adolescents. The Graduate School of Education at the University of Leiden supported the time necessary to revise my very rough original draft; I owe special thanks to M. vanIJzendoorn and A. Bus for their support and hospitality. My home institution, the University of Georgia, also provided support of various kinds, but especially the encouragement to do what they saw as interesting work; Bill McKillup and George M. A. Stanic, of the Department of Elementary Education, and Abraham Tesser and my other colleagues at the Institute for Behavioral Research, deserve special mention both for providing support and for their useful critical commentary on this body of work.

The schools where I conducted my research on children were obviously important, for without the support of principals, teachers, children, and parents this work never would have gotten beyond the discussion stage. I acknowledge the following people and schools in Athens: the McPhaul Child and Family Development Center at the University of Georgia (UGA), Tom Davis and the teachers of the Timothy Road Elementary School, Sherri Malone and the teachers at Barnett Shoals Elementary School, Lola Finn and the teachers at the Whit Davis Elementary School, and Caroline Riddlehuber and the teachers at the Athens Academy Middle Schools. In White County, Georgia, Tom and Sarah Kennedy made the impossible task of coping with a data collection site 80 miles away, relatively easy to handle. I also wish to thank Patti Davis Huberty, whose initial class project with me turned into something very special and interesting. In Sheffield the Head Teachers at the Uppperthorpe and Prince Edward Middle Schools were most supportive of work they saw as having real relevance to their students.

Another group that has consistently recognized the importance of recess and playground activity is the National Association of Elementary School Principals (NAESP). Lee Green, the editor of *Principal*, has consistently encouraged the dissemination of research in this area. Related to the NAESP, are the numerous teachers, parents, and principals who have shared their concerns with me over the diminishing role of recess in schools. These folk are working hard to systematically gather data on the role of recess in school. Christine Edwards, of Tarpon Springs, FL, for example, shared the national survey of recess that she and the NAESP conducted. The energy and commitment of this group is inspirational.

Lastly, my wife and children must be acknowledged. Of course my children provide me with my most direct tutorials in rough-and-tumble play. They attest to the value of play, vigorously! Lee Galda, as always, is my sounding board, providing valued and insightful feedback on all aspects of my work.

1

Children on the Playground at Recess: What's So Important?*

Introduction

The topic of this book—what children do on playgrounds during their recess periods—may seem an unlikely one for an academic work. After all, what children do on playgrounds is typically not considered important by most teachers and parents, and certainly not by scholars. This disregard for the playground, as we will see throughout this volume, is reflected in the paucity of empirical research on the topic. A notable exception to this statement is the recent volume edited by Craig Hart (1993a). While disregard for recess may typify most of those in the social science community, recess is important to a number of people, especially children, and of increasing importance to teachers, administrators, and parents.

As I see it, as a parent, a former primary school teacher, and a researcher, the recess period represents an almost unique part of the school day. By this I mean it is one of the few times when children can interact with their peers on their own terms with minimal adult intervention. Consequently, the playground represents one of the few places in primary and middle schools to observe spontaneous peer interaction. Classrooms, generally, do not have much spontaneous peer interation! So, from a scientific perspective, recess represents a unique opportunity to study children's social interaction.

Recess and playground behavior is also interesting from an educational policy perspective. While recess exists in some form in most primary schools, its role in the school curriculum, is currently being questioned. Thus, research in this area, beside being very interesting, also has real policy implications. In the remainder of this chapter I will outline what I see as the important issues in this area.

---

*This chapter is an expanded version of a paper written with P. K. Smith.

What Is Recess?

School recess, or play time, is a break period, typically held outdoors, for children. Generally, children in schools from preschool through the elementary school level have recess as a scheduled part of their day. Recess periods tend not to exist in schools for adolescents, such as junior high and middle schools.

Although some form of recess is almost always present in elementary schools, the number of recess periods per day, the duration of the period(s), and the supervisory policy for recess periods typically varies greatly from one school to another. For example, in some British primary schools children have three outdoor play periods per day: morning and afternoon periods of about 15 minutes each and a dinner play period of about 80 to 90 minutes. In American elementary schools the length of the period and its placement in the school day also varies by individual school.

Additionally, the nature of supervision of children while they are on the playground varies widely. In some schools teachers are expected to supervise children during recess periods, while in other schools—even schools within the same city/school district—this task is often relegated to paraprofessionals, or to other adults who have little or no special training for the task. In short, recess is ubiquitous to the extent that most preschool and primary school children experience it as part of their school day. What they experience, however, varies widely from school to school. Generally, there is no explicit school policy, either at the school or local levels, regarding recess. The closest thing that resembles such a policy might be school or local rules regarding aggression and bullying that may take place on the playground (see Ladd & Price, 1993, and Olweus, 1993, for extended discussions of this issue). This general lack of policy for such a common and sometimes lengthy period is puzzling. In the next section the results of a national survey on recess periods conducted by the National Association of Elementary School Principals (NAESP) will be presented.

A National Survey of Recess

In 1989 the NAESP conducted a national survey on recess practices in America. (I am extremely grateful to Christine Edwards of Tarpon Springs, FL, who compiled, summarized, and provided these data.) This survey was conducted because no such data existed! The survey was sent to 51 state superintendents of school (including the superintendent for Washington, D.C.) and responses were received from 47 states. The ubiquity of recess was substantiated by the survey: 90 percent of the school districts had some form of recess. In 96 percent of the cases recess occurred once or twice per day. Recess lasted 15 to 20 minutes in 75 percent of the cases. Data regarding supervisory practices for recess periods indicates that teachers were supervisors in 50 percent of the cases, while teacher aides supervised children in 36 percent of the cases. Of the aides, 86 percent received no formal training for supervising recess. The locus for recess policy decisions in 87 percent of the cases was within the specific school. Relatedly, recess policy was about evenly divided regarding structured versus unstructured recess periods.

In short, recess is a staple in schools. Schools themselves (that is, teachers and principals) make recess policy and the policy is equally divided between structured and unstructured periods. The structured recess periods must be very interesting when they are supervised by aides, who typically are untrained in matters pertaining to recess!

The Recess Controversy

The role of recess in schools has been recently questioned (see Hart, 1993a, 1993b, and Sutton-Smith, 1990). Embedded in the larger context of the "effective education" debate teachers and parents have been questioning the role of recess in the school day (see the *New York Times*, 8 January 1989). Sides in a pro-recess and anti-recess debate have been drawn. Two main reasons are normally addressed by those opposed to recess (see Blatchford, 1988). First, it is argued by the antis that recess detracts from needed instructional time in an already crowded and long school day. Further, antis argue that recess periods, often arbitrarily placed in the school schedule, disrupt children's sustained work patterns. The second anti-recess argument commonly advanced is that recess encourages aggression and antisocial behavior on the playground. This point will be given extensive treatment in the present volume, though it has been reviewed elsewhere (see Blatchford, 1988; Evans, 1989; Smith & Thompson, 1991). Suffice it to say for the time being that aggression on elementary and middle school playgrounds is very uncommon, accounting for less than 2 or 3 percent of children's total behavior.

The issue of loss of instructional time is related to a specific dimension of recess behavior—children's physical activity—to the extent that recess is seen by educators as either providing opportunity to vent "excess energy" or exciting children to such high levels that they become inattentive, making effective class work difficult. While systematic data on this issue, as on most aspects of recess, are limited, Blatchford (1988) provides anecdotal evidence from British teachers that *both* supports and undermines this argument. Some teachers suggest that recess gives children a much needed break from their work, while other teachers complain that it is disruptive. According to recess critics, task-oriented children are forced to leave their work to take recess and return distracted. Clearly, the variation in recess forms discussed above may be responsible for this state of confusion. This issue will be addressed specifically in a later chapter.

The pro-recess arguments are almost mirror images of the antis arguments (see Sutton-Smith, 1990, for an alternative view). Generally, proponents of recess offer some folk variant of surplus energy theory whereby children need recess to "blow off steam"; this reasoning is used by parents and educators in Australia (Evans, 1989), Britain (Blatchford, 1988), and America (Parrott, 1975; Pellegrini, 1989). The argument goes something like this: when children sit still for prolonged periods of time they accumulate surplus energy; therefore physical activity in recess is necessary to "blow off," or use up, this surplus energy so that the children can then concentrate on the more sedentary tasks of the classroom. The evidence given for this surplus energy theory is scientifically questionable, and typically involves examples of children fidgeting in their seats and generally showing lower levels of attention as a function of confinement time.

The empirical record for these issues is sparse indeed. In what follows, empirical research that bears on the role of recess in schools will be briefly reviewed. This topic will be given more thorough treatment in subsequent chapters. It should be stressed here that much of this research was *not* designed to address these specific questions; instead, it was designed to address other, related issues.

An important school-level variable, playground design, will be briefly reviewed here and discussed in greater depth in Chapter 2. Next, I will review research that has examined variables that affect children's behavior on the playground at recess; I will consider both child-level variables (i.e., gender and preference for outdoors, temperament, and age) and school-level variables (i.e., recess timing). While I recognize that such a dichotomy between the child-level and school-level variables is artificial, I will present them separately for reasons of clarity.

Playground Design Effects

The relation between playground design and children's behavior has been studied at both the community (Naylor, 1985) and the school level (Frost, 1986; Hart & Sheehan, 1986). The school-level studies, with the exception of Hart and Sheehan, examine the extent to which children choose to play in certain play areas and the types of behavior exhibited while there. That children self-selected themselves into those play areas prevents a discussion of "effects" of playground design.

Frost (1986) and colleagues compared primary school children's behaviors on traditional, contemporary, and adventure playgrounds. They found that children were equally cooperative on all types of playscapes but exhibited more fantasy play on adventure playgrounds and more functional play on traditional playgrounds. These results are not consistent with studies in which children's exposure to specific playground designs was experimentally manipulated (Hart & Sheenan, 1986). *Within* contemporary playscapes, there is also significant variation. In short, children act very differently on different types on playscapes. As I will illustrate below, other variables also affect children's recess behavior.

Child Variables Affecting Recess Behavior

Gender and Indoor or Outdoor Preference

That boys are more physically active than girls is well documented (Eaton & Enns, 1986). These differences, often discussed in terms of temperament, are observed from infancy through childhood, though a decrement of activity as a function of age is observed in later childhood (Eaton & Yu, 1989). Further, higher levels of physical activity are elicited in low, as compared to high, spatial density environments (Smith & Connolly, 1980). That is, children are more active in spacious, as compared to restricted, environments. These two findings could be responsible for the fact that, given free choice, boys, more often than girls, prefer to go outdoors for recess. Where free choice does not exist, girls, when asked, would rather stay in than go out; boys, on the other hand, prefer to go out (Blatchford, 1988; Boulton & Smith, 1993; Lever, 1976; Serbin, Marchessault, McAffer, Peters, & Schwartzmann, 1993). This gender-related preference for outdoor play has been documented by means of behavioral observations during the preschool period (Harper & Sander,

1975) and during early adolescence (See Chapter 8 below; also see Serbin et al., 1993) and by means of questionnaires during the elementary school years (Blatchford, 1988).

Boys' preference for outdoor play is often explained in terms of their biological predisposition, or temperament, for high levels of activity (Harper & Sanders, 1975). This line of reasoning would lead to the hypothesis that boys, more than girls, should be more active both on the playground and in the classroom. Boys' activity level, according to this hypothesis, should be of higher intensity and longer duration than the activity levels of girls. Behavioral observations of boys' playground behavior are consistent with this hypothesis; for example, boys from the preschool through early adolescence periods engage in more vigorous physical activity, such as rough-and-tumble play and other forms of vigorous play, than do girls (Boulton & Smith, 1993; Humphreys & Smith, 1984; Ladd & Price, 1993; Maccoby & Jacklin, 1987; also see Chapters 6, 7, and 8 in this volume). Regarding physical activity in classrooms, boys are considered by their teachers to be more destructive and less attentive than girls (Serbin, Zelkowitz, Doyle, & Gold, 1990).

There are alternate explanations for these gender-related differences. Specifically, boys and girls may differentially prefer outdoor play because of socialization issues (Serbin et al., 1993). For example, girls may prefer indoor to outdoor play spaces because they are less likely to be disturbed indoors. That is, when boys and girls are on the playground together boys, because of their high levels of activity and their games, may intrude into girls' play spaces. Indeed, Maccoby and Jacklin (1987) proffer this as a reason for preschoolers' gender segregation. Anecdotal evidence presented by Blatchford (1988) suggests that girls and young children dislike outdoor play because boys, particularly older boys, invade their space with balls and charging bodies. Rather than reducing preference for outdoor play to a biological or social origin, it probably makes sense to consider these aspects of gender as being due to the interaction between socialization and hormonal events.

An interesting test of this hypothesis would be to examine outdoor preference at an all-girls school with age-segregated recess periods, where such intrusions do not exist; I would predict that girls' choice of outdoor play would increase. Restrictions on boys' vigorous games, like football, should also have this effect. Regarding alternate explanations for gender differences in classroom behavior, such differences are typically confounded by the gender of the teachers, who are often female. It is quite possible that female teachers react differently to active behavior in boys versus girls.

We thus have reasonably good data that boys, more than girls, prefer outdoor play because of their propensity for physical activity. Preference for physical activity often varies also as a function of children's temperament and age.

The Roles of Temperament and Age in Children's Recess Behavior

Temperament is a construct used to describe relatively stable individual differences in children that have an early origin and a biological component. Children's physical activity, as I noted above, has often been treated as a dimension of temperament and can be measured behavioral, using direct observations or mechanical recorders, or by parent- or teacher-completed checklists. Behavioral observations, of course, are both expensive and time consuming. Eaton and Yu (1989) have found that teachers' rank orderings of children in terms of their motoric activity correlates very well ($r = .69$) with motion recorder measures.

To my knowledge, no empirical research has been conducted on the relation between children's temperament and their recess behavior, per se. Clearly, such research is needed. For example, it may be that children who are temperamentally very active have a greater "need" for recess than less active children. We do know that negative associations exist between children's activity level and self-direction in classrooms (see Martin, 1988, for a summary of temperament and classroom research). Further, we know that the longer children sit in classrooms the less attentive they become; these same inattentive children tend to be active on the playground at recess (see Chapter 5). It may be that making a provision for recess after specific periods of seat work would increase the attention of active children.

Age is another related, child-level moderator variable to the extent that physical activity seems to decline during the elementary school years (Eaton & Yu, 1989). Consequently, children's "need" for outdoor recess may decline with age. The research finding that children, as they move through adolescence, less frequently choose to play outdoors (see Chapters 9 and 10) supports this proposition. Further, gender and age seem to have interactive effects on physical activity observed on the playground at recess. Gender differences for preschool children's vigorous behavior on the playground were not observed by Smith and Hagan (1980) whereas there were significant gender differences observed by Pellegrini and Davis (see Chapter 5) in a sample of 9-year-old school children. Multiage studies, preferably longitudinal studies, where moderator variables like temperament and gender can be tracked across childhood will be necessary to address this age and gender interaction more thoroughly.

Thus, children's behavior on the playground at recess is moderated by a number of child-level variables. These child-level variables, however, interact with aspects of the larger school environment.

School-Level Variables Affecting Playground Behavior

If a poll were conducted with a large sample of professional educators and parents, asking them why recess should be included in the school curriculum, the most commonly voiced rationale would probably relate to some aspect of "surplus energy theory," such as children needing recess to "blow off steam." The validity of surplus energy theory is questionable (Smith & Hagan, 1980), for it is based on outmoded concepts linking energy and motivation. However, the idea that children may "need" or benefit from periodic changes from sedentary class work is both reasonable and rooted in other, more current, psychological theories, such as Fagen's (1981) deprivation theory of play and Berlyne's (1966) novelty theory of play. The effect of recess timing, or the amount of time that children are expected to work at their seats before going out to recess, on children's behavior has been addressed in two experimental field studies using within subjects research designs. Both these studies assumed that children's physical activity would vary as a function of their previous confinement to a sedentary environment.

Smith and Hagan (1980) studied three and four year olds in two English nursery classes. The children stayed in the classroom for shorter (45 mins.) or longer (90 mins.) periods before going outdoors for recess. Smith and Hagan based their hypotheses on the idea that the motivation for active physical play could increase as a function of deprivation. The indoor-classroom conditions were organized such that active play was almost entirely prevented. The hypotheses were supported: children were more active (level of intensity) for a longer period (duration) after the longer, compared to the shorter, confinement periods. Further, a decrement of activity on the playground was observed as a function of time spent outdoors. No gender differences were observed. The study suggested that confinement resulted in increased physical activity; physical activity, in turn, decreased as a function of time exercising.

Extending this approach to older children, Pellegrini and Davis (reported in full in Chapter 5) examined the effects of confinement on 9-year-old boys' and girls' classroom *and* playground behavior in an American elementary school. As in the Smith and Hagan study, children were confined for shorter and longer periods and the duration and intensity of their playground behavior was observed. Pellegrini and Davis also found the confinement increased the intensity of children's playground activity. They found significant gender effects at this older age: boys were more active on the playground than were girls, particularly after the longer confinement period. Further, frequency and levels of active behavior of the boys decreased as a function of time on the playground. These results support the general model outlined above: boys are more active on the playground than are girls, and their levels of activity can be increased by previously limiting their opportunity for vigorous physical activity.

This line of inquiry, though preliminary, has important implications for future research and educational policy. One pressing question for educators is determining the optimal length for recess periods. We have very little information on this topic. This information would be valuable in terms of theory (play deprivation theory and arousal theory would predict a decrement of activity in recess as a function of time) and certainly valuable for educational policy. The findings of Pellegrini and Davis suggest that children's active play at recess does not last very long; there are marked decreases after the first six or seven minutes. Future work should document the specific duration of active play and how it varies as a function of the age and gender of children, their previous confinement, and the length of the recess period.

From a policy perspective, it seems important to answer these questions in order to design recess periods that maximize benefits, in terms of subsequent attention in class, and minimize children's boredom on the playground. The anecdotal evidence provided by Blatchford (1989), from both educators and children in Britain, suggests that dinner/lunch play of over one hour is too long, to the extent that children become bored and sometimes aggressive toward the end of these periods.

However, duration of play periods and play bouts alone does not address the whole issue of possible benefits of physical activity exhibited at recess, especially if one is concerned with the physical exercise dimensions of recess. It is probably true that high-intensity physical play bouts are characterized by short durations. Some of the literature on training of muscle strength and cardiac capacity suggests that short but intense periods are more effective than longer, less-intensive periods (Bekoff, 1988). Relatedly, it may be that children's attention can be maximized by encouraging short, but frequent, physically active bouts. This is clearly an area in which more work is needed.

Measurement Issues

The measurement of duration and intensity of physical activity has attracted much attention. Of course, behavioral observation of these aspects of activity is the most accurate, yet also the most time-consuming, method. While there are many objective measures of activity intensity, like actometers (Eaton, Enns, & Presse, 1987) and heart rate (Dauncey & James, 1979), they are both obtrusive and time consuming to use. Recently, researchers have developed observational checklists that correlate highly with these more direct measures, and that are more economical to use as well as yielding duration measures. These schemes generally code body posture—for example, lying, sitting, or standing (Eaton, Enns, & Presse, 1987) or the part of the body engaged in activity (upper or lower; Hovell, Bursick, Sharkey, & McClure, 1978); intensity is then coded along three dimensions (high, medium, and low). Maccoby and Jacklin (1987) used a 7-point scale to code intensity; the 3-point scale yields less information but may be more reliable for observers to use. Martin and Bateson (1988) suggest that agreement on intensity ratings, while difficult, can be maximized if ratings correspond to the number of features present; for example, a low intensity rating would have 2 features and a high rating would have 8. Similar intensity ratings have been applied to children's level of fidgeting and concentration in classroom tasks (see Chapter 5). Duration of activity is derived by multiplying these codes by the number of intervals in which they are observed.

In short, there are reliable and valid measures of children's physically active play that can easily be applied to their recess behavior. Their use should be expanded in our studies of recess, for children's activity level is certainly an important aspect of recess.

The Educational Implications of Recess

Because recess is embedded in school, the question of its educational role is sometimes voiced (see Hart, 1993b). "Educational role" typically refers to the cognitive implications of recess. We can also include a broader definition of educational implications, touching on issues of social competence, such as popularity with peers. To adapt successfully to schools, children must function in both social and cognitive spheres; indeed, the two are intercorrelated (see Chapter 5). I will consider children's cognitive and social outcomes as an appropriate measure for the educational impact of recess.

Cognitive Outcomes

Researchers interested in relations between recess behavior and traditional cognitive outcome measures, such as school achievement, can generally be put into two categories. The first category includes researchers, typically adherents of arousal theory, who suggest that the physical activity exhibited during recess has important cognitive consequences; for example, the physical activity of adults has been shown to relate to immediate increases in attention (Tomporowski & Ellis, 1986). Research with schoolage children, on the other hand, is not consistent with the adult results. We (see Chapter 5) found that vigorous play at recess was negatively related to attention on a postrecess achievement task, while sedentary playground behavior was positively correlated with attention and negatively correlated with fidgeting. These results suggest that vigorous activity can actually interfere with the subsequent attention of some children. While more research and replication is needed, these results suggest that opportunities for vigorous play actually exacerbate active children's classroom inattention.

It may be that these children need changes from seat work, but changes that are settling rather than exciting. Drawing on adult findings, it may also be the case that specific types of vigorous activity interact statistically with type of cognitive task. Another possibility is that children need some form of "cool-down" time after recess. A Taiwanese student of mine, Juimien Ku Chang, informs me that in Taiwan where there are numerous recess periods per day, children are given five to six minutes of transition time between entering the room after recess until they are expected to sit down and engage in their academic tasks. While I know of no more general empirical support for this claim, it makes intuitive sense and certainly merits study.

Another possibility is that physical activity per se at recess is not the most important variable relating to subsequent improved attention in the classroom. Following novelty theory (Berlyne, 1966), children may habituate to stimuli, like school tasks and indeed recess time, as a function of familiarity and time; physical activity might then be just one of many ways in which children seek novelty. For example, sedentary social interaction provides a change from typical classrooms regimens to the extent that children can choose a peer with whom to interact on their own terms. Recess provides opportunities for this form of behavior. I found that nonsocial sedentary behavior decreased as a function of recess time but social sedentary behavior increased across time (see Chapter 5). Thus, optimal length of recess period may vary, depending on our desired behavior. Shorter periods may be better for physical activity, but longer periods may be necessary before children habituate to social sedentary activities.

Another interesting, and potentially important, aspect of this research relates to the type of tasks on which children are observed before and after recess. Classrooms vary in terms of requirements for concentration, social interaction, and sedentary activity; these factors may interact with corresponding dimensions of recess experience. Other task-specific measures, like motivation to work on specific tasks, may also affect attention. For example, there may be reliable task attention differences as a function of gender preference for specific tasks. It may be that boys attend to and participate in male preferred tasks, like mathematics and block play, while girls are more attentive in linguistic and dramatic play contexts (Pellegrini & Perlmutter, 1989). Of course, these gender-related differences interact, in turn, with age as children's behavior becomes more sex-role stereotyped. Future research investigating these interactive effects is clearly necessary. For example, experimental studies that examine age × gender × task effects in relation to recess variables would help clarify these issues.

The cognitive implications of children's recess behavior have also been studied from the point of view that children's cognition is facilitated by social interaction with peers. The theoretical orientations in this area can be traced to Humphrey's (1976) idea of the social origins of intelligence and to Piaget's (1970) equilibration theory whereby peer interaction facilitates cognitive conflict and subsequent re-equilibration. Following Piagetian theory, I examined the extent to which the social behavior of kindergarten children on the school playground during recess predicted their achievement in first grade (see Chapter 6). Of specific interest was the relative roles of peer and adult interaction for children's cognitive development. The results were consistent with the Piagetian model in that a facilitative role of peers and an inhibitive role of adults were found. Specifically, interactions with adults and with peers on the playground at recess were, respectively, negative and positive predictors of first grade achievement. These measures of kindergarten playground behavior accounted for a significant amount of the variance in first grade achievement, even when kindergarten achievement was controlled. In short, what children do on the playground does have cognitive implications. Further, these behaviors seem to provide significantly more insight into children's functioning than do traditional measures of cognition.

While these results are consistent with theory, they should be interpreted cautiously as they are based on a few studies with limited sample sizes. Further, the measures of social interaction were rather gross. I coded children's social behavior as peer-directed or adult-directed and whether children were talking or not talking. Clearly these variables are "packaged" variables to the extent that they include numerous subvariables that probably relate differentially to cognition. Future research should use specific theoretically relevant measures of social interaction as predictors of cognitive status. For example, Humphrey's (1976) theory suggests that diversity of social experience is important for intellectual growth; the variety of roles and behaviors that children exhibit with various partners could be used as predictors in future research. From a Piagetian perspective, children's conflicts and conflict resolutions could be coded.

Additionally, it is probably important to consider the extent to which interactions with peers and adults are reciprocal (i.e., where roles are changes and power is shared) or complementary (i.e., where expert-novice power relationships are maintained) (Hinde, 1987). Clearly, children can and do engage in reciprocal and complementary interactions with adults (when they play and are taught, respectively) and with peers. Thus, equilibration theory would predict reciprocal interactions to be important in children's social cognitive development. In short, the extant data tells us that social interaction has important cognitive implications. The time has come to test more specific theories of the ways in which this operates.

Social Outcomes

The notion that recess behavior is important for children's socialization has a long history (See Sutton-Smith, 1981, 1990, for summaries). While much of this work concerns children on playgrounds, *not* in school settings specifically, a number of school playground studies do exist and they will be the focus of this section. The studies reviewed vary in terms of specificity of the outcomes measures considered, from the global consideration of "social skills necessary for adult life" (Sluckin, 1981, p. 2) and adult roles and occupational choice (Finan, 1982; Lever, 1976), to specific measures of peer cooperation (Pellegrini, 1992) and popularity (Ladd, 1983; Ladd & Price, 1993). We will begin with the global and move toward the specific.

Sluckin (1981) spent two years observing children in British primary, and middle schools. He concluded that there were similarities between the strategies and roles used and taken by children and adults. He noted that the facial gestures used by children to exhibit dominance are similar to those used by adults. Relatedly, Sluckin spent considerable effort explicating the ways in which children used ritual as a way in which to resolve conflict without violence. While adults do not face the likelihood of violence frequently, they too resort to ritual as a way in which to exhibit dominance. Sluckin, like Sutton-Smith (1971) before him, considers the social skills learned on the playground as important for later development. Indeed, they both argue that the context of play with peers is a unique one for learning social skills to the extent that the playful and nonserious tenor allows children to experiment with new and novel social strategies. Children also learn skills of presentation management (e.g., keeping their status even after loosing a game) and manipulation (e.g., ways of excluding unwanted children from a game). These social strategies are certainly not taught in most classrooms.

The notion of recess play as preparation for adulthood is extended to the development of sex roles. Sluckin, for example, notes that the family-oriented and competitive games that girls and boys played, respectively, may prepare them for their corresponding adult gender roles. Similarly, Lever (1976), in her observational study of fifth graders on the playground at recess, suggests that the play and games of children on the school playground contribute to traditional sex role divisions. Lever found, like Harper and Sanders and Pellegrini (see Chapter 8), that boys, more than girls, preferred outdoor, public play, while girls preferred indoor, more private play. Second, boys, more than girls, played in larger and more age-heterogeneous groups. Their play often involved coordinating the different types of children around a competitive, team theme. These games, Lever argued, prepare boys for adult leadership roles. Girls' play was more often cooperative than competitive and occurred in smaller, less diverse groups. When girls played with younger children, the older girls typically accommodated to the play of the younger children. Also, girls engaged in more close and intimate relationships in their small groups. Thus, argues Lever, girls are learning to nurture in the playground; this, in turn, prepares them for latter childcare duties.

In the work of Sluckin and Lever the socialization model is prevalent. They believe that children's roles are the product of adult roles and suggest that children's play reflects these roles, generally. Thus, as the role of women in American society changes, so too should the sex-role play of children. While this theory seems reasonable, so too is the notion that children's play is not only imitative but also creative, and that in turn, it affects their later development. Indeed, a long-standing criticism of socialization models is that the effect of society on children's social development is conceptualized as unidirectional, whereas individual differences in children, such as temperament and sociometric status, and the resources available to them actually mediate societal demands on children (Bronfenbrenner, 1979; MacDonald, 1993).

A study by Ladd (1983) of the recess behavior of third and fourth grade boys and girls clearly illustrates these "child effects." I noted above that boys' play groups are larger, or more extensive, than girls' groups. Ladd (1983) found that boys' and girls' social networks varied according to their sociometric status such that rejected children, regardless of gender, played in smaller groups than popular or average children; gender differences in the expected direction were observed for popular and average children. Further, the diversity of children played with at recess is affected by both gender and sociometric status; for example, while girls spent more time, compared to boys, interacting with same-gender playmates, rejected boys, compared to other types of boys, spent a significant portion of their time playing with girls (Ladd, 1983). Thus, the way in which boys and girls interact on the playground is influenced by both gender and individual difference variables. That boys and girls merely reproduce dominant cultural values on the playground seems too simplistic; individual differences interact with broader societal norms to effect the ways in which they play at recess.

In both the Sluckin and Lever studies the social implications, or functions, of children's behavior on the school playground was supported by implicit argument-from-design features. That is, similarities between the behavioral and structural features of the playground and adult roles were described. While this is an interesting, and indeed a necessary first step, en route to establishing the functional significance of a behavior, hypothesized associations between recess behavior and social outcomes measures must be tested more directly. Indeed, the Ladd (1983) study illustrated the ways in which such an empirical study can add to our understanding of the meaning of children's recess behavior. There are a few other studies of this kind, some of which also consider the ways in which individual differences in children mediate social development.

I will review studies using both contemporaneous and longitudinal correlations relevant to the implications of recess. Contemporaneous analyses, obviously, prohibit one from making functional, or causal, statements. Longitudinal correlational and experimental studies are necessary for getting at causation. Simple correlational studies are interesting, however, to the extent that they inform us that something important *may* be going on. That is, statistically significant correlation coefficients suggest that one behavior results in learning or developing another behavior. More conservatively, it may also mean that one has already attained a certain skill and that the occurrence of a correlated behavior indicates that one is practicing that skill. In either case, whether learning or practice, the correlation has educational meaning.

In separate studies Pellegrini (see Chapters 6 and 7) found that the recess behavior of elementary school children related to their ability to solve hypothetical social problems and to their teachers' judgments regarding their antisocial personality. Again, these relations varied in terms of both the gender and sociometric status of the children. Girls who engaged in physically vigorous behaviors, such as running, swinging, and rough play, like play fighting (see Chapter 7), were considered to be antisocial by their teachers; the same was not true for boys. It may be, following Lever and Sluckin, that teachers too considered the playground as a place for children to learn sex-role stereotyped behaviors. Those violating these norms were considered deviant. Relatedly, the rough play of rejected, but not popular, children (both boys and girls) related positively and significantly to their antisocial rating by teachers. In this case, the correspondence between the two measures may reflect the fact that rejected children actually are antisocial (as evidenced by behavioral observations). Certainly, future studies should separate gender and sociometric effects.

Longitudinal work on rough play and antisocial personality ratings clarifies, to some degree, issues related to directionality, but gender and sociometric status are still confounded. I (see Chapter 6) found that kindergarten children's aggression on the playground was a significant predictor of their being considered antisocial by their first grade teacher; children's kindergarten antisocial status was controlled so that the unique contribution of aggression, independent of a stable antisocial personality, could be assessed. This finding, while limited to the extent that children's gender and sociometric status were not considered, has important implications to the extent that the playground at recess is used as a venue by some children to be aggressive and antisocial. This is consistent with Whitney and Smith's (in press) work on bullying, which suggests that when bullying does occur, the most likely venue, especially in primary schools, is the school playground. This illustrates the darker side to recess. Some children do use recess as a place to be aggressive and to bully their classmates, even though this may be infrequent in absolute terms. Further research on the role of various antibullying programs in schools is needed (e.g., Olweus, 1993; Smith & Thompson, 1991).

We have similar results and problems with the next set of findings for correlations between playground behavior and social problem-solving ability. Significant and positive correlations between rough play and social problem solving are reported for boys, but not for girls (see Chapter 7), and for popular, but not for rejected, children. These sociometric status results were replicated in a longitudinal study whereby the rough play of popular, not rejected, elementary school students predicted social problem solving one year later, while controlling for year 1 social problem-solving status (Pellegrini, 1991).

To summarize, children's recess does have educational implications. In both correlational and longitudinal research, children's recess behavior is related, in theoretically predictable ways, to both cognitive and social outcome measures. Children's gender and sociometric status seem particularly important as mediators for recess effects. However, much more research, preferably longitudinal, needs to be carried out to clarify the causal relations and to put the findings obtained so far on a firm basis.

Conclusion

Given the importance of the topic, there is a relative paucity of empirical research on children's recess. This lack of descriptive and predictive work is indeed surprising in light of the ubiquity of recess in school curricula. The research that does exist, however, tells a rather consistent story. Timing and duration of recess relates to playground activity, and possibly to subsequent classroom behavior, in ways that interact with age, gender, and temperament. Recess behavior is also a generally positive predictor of children's, and especially boys', social cognitive development. Thus, it is seems to have educational value and certainly has considerable educational relevance. There are clear lines of future research which could be both theoretically interesting and practically important.

References

Bekoff, M. (1988). Social play and physical training: When "Not enough" may be plenty. *Ethology, 20,* 1-4.

Berlyne, D. (1966). Curiousity and exploration. *Science, 153,* 25-33.

Blatchford, P. (1988). *Playtime in the primary school.* Windsor, U.K.: NFER-Nelson.

Boulton, M., & Smith, P. K. (1993). Ethnic, gender partner, and activity preferences in mixed-race playgrounds in the UK. In C. Hart (ed.), *Children on playgrounds* (pp. 210-238). Albany, NY: SUNY Press.

Bronfenbrenner, U. (1979). *The ecology of human development.* Cambridge, MA: Harvard University Press.

Dauncey, M., & James, W. (1979). Assessment of heart rate method for determining energy expenditure in man, using a whole body calimeter. *British Journal of Nutition, 42,* 1-13.

Eaton, W., & Enns, L. (1986). Sex differences in human motor activity level. *Psychological Bulletin, 100,* 19-28.

Eaton, W., Enns, L., & Presse, M. (1987). Scheme for observing activity. *Journal of Psychoeducational Assessment, 3,* 273-280.

Eaton, W., & Yu, A. (1989). Are sex differences in child motor activity level a function of sex differences in maturational status? *Child Development, 60,* 1005-1011.

Evans, J. (1989). *Children at play: Life in the school playground.* Geelong, Australia: Deakin University Press.

Fagen, R. (1981). *Animal play behavior.* New York: Oxford University Press.

Finnan, C. (1982). The ethnography of children's spontaneous play. In G. Spindler (ed.), *Doing the ethnography of schooling* (pp. 355-381). New York: Holt, Rinehart, and Winston.

Harper, L., & Sanders, K. (1975). Preschool children's use of space: Sex differences in outdoor play. *Developmental Psychology,11*, 119.

Hart, C. (Ed.). (1993a). *Children on playgrounds*. Albany, NY: SUNY Press.

————. (1993b). Children on playgrounds: Applying current knowledge to future practice and inquiry. In C. Hart (ed.), *Children on playgrounds* (pp. 418-432). Albany, NY: SUNY Press.

————. (1993c). Introduction: Toward a further understanding of children's development on playgrounds. In C. Hart (ed.), *Children on playgrounds* (pp. 1-12). Albany, NY: SUNY Press.

Hinde, R. (1987). *Individuals, relationships and culture*. London: Cambridge University Press.

Hovell, M., Bursick, J., Sharkey, R., & McClure, J. (1978). An evaluation of elementary students' voluntary physical activity during recess. *Research Quarterly for Exercise and Sport, 69*, 460-474.

Humphreys, A., & Smith, P. K. (1984). Rough-and-tumble play in preschool and playground. In P. K. Smith (ed.), *Play in animals and humans* (pp. 241-270). Oxford: Blackwell.

Ladd, G. (1983). Social networks of popular, average, and rejected children in school settings. *Merrill-Palmer Quarterly, 29*, 283-307.

Ladd, G., & Price, J. (1993). Playstyles of peer-accepted and peer-rejected children on the playground. In C. Hart (ed.), *Children on playgrounds* (pp. 130-161). Albany, NY: SUNY Press.

Lever, J. (1976). Sex differences in the games children play. *Social Problems, 23*, 478-487.

Maccoby, E., & Jacklin, C. (1987). Gender segregation in childhood. In H. Reese (ed.), *Advances in child development and behavior* (pp. 239-287). New York: Academic Press.

MacDonald, K. (1993). Introduction. In K. MacDonald (ed.), *Parents and children playing*. Albany, NY: SUNY Press.

Martin, P., & Bateson, P. (1988). *Measuring behaviour*. London: Cambridge University Press.

Martin, R. (1988). Child temperament and educational outcomes. In A. D. Pellegrini (ed.), *Psychological bases for early education* (pp. 185-206). Chichester, U.K.:Wiley.

Olweus, D. (1993). Bullies on the playground. In C. Hart (ed.), *Children on playgrounds* (pp. 85-128). Albany, NY: SUNY Press.

Parrott, S. (1975). Games children play: Ethnography of a second grade recess. In J. Spradley & D. McCardy (eds.), *The cultural experience* (pp. 207-219). Palo Alto, CA: SRA.

Pellegrini, A. D. (1988). Elementary school children's rough-and-tumble play and social competence. *Developmental Psychology, 24,* 802-806.

———. (1989). Elementary school children's rough-and-tumble play. *Early Childhood Research Quarterly, 4,* 245-260.

———. (1991). A longitudinal study of popular and rejected children's rough-and-tumble play. *Early Education and Development, 3,* 205-213.

———. (1992). Kindergarten children's social cognitive status as a predictor of first grade achievement. *Early Childhood Research Quarterly, 7,* 565-577.

Pellegrini, A. D., & Davis, P. (1993). Confinement effects on playground and classroom behavior. *British Journal of Educational Psychology, 33,* 88-95.

Pellegrini, A., & Perlmutter, J. (1989). Classroom contextual effects on children's play. *Developmental Psychology, 25,* 289-296.

Serbin, L., Marchessault, K. McAffer, V., Peters, P., & Schwartzman, A. (1993). Patterns of behavior on the playground in 9- to 11-year-old girls and boys. In C. Hart (ed.), *Children on playgrounds* (pp. 162-183). Albany, NY: SUNY Press.

Serbin, L., Zelkowitz, P., Doyle, A., & Gold, D. (1990). The socialization of sex-differentiated skills and academic performance. *Sex Roles, 23,* 613-628.

Smith, P. K., & Connolly, K. (1980). *The ecology of preschool behavior.* New York: Cambridge University Press.

Smith, P. K., & Hagan, T. (1980). Effects of deprivation on exercise of nursery school children. *Animal Behaviour, 28,* 922-928.

Smith, P. K., & Thompson, D. (Eds.). (1991). *Practical approaches to bullying.* London: Fulton.

Sutton-Smith, B. (1971). A syntax for play and games. In R. Herron & B. Sutton-Smith (eds.), *Child's play* (pp. 298-310). New York: Wiley.

———. (1981). *A history of children's play.* Philadelphia: University of Pennsylvania Press.

———. (1990). School playground as festival. *Children's Environment Quarterly, 7,* 3-7.

Tomporowski, P., & Ellis, N. (1986). Effects of exercise on cognitive processes: A review. *Psychological Bulletin, 99*, 338-346.

Whitney, I., & Smith, P. K. (in press). A survey of the nature and extent of bully/victim problems in junior/middle and secondary schools, *Educational Research.*

2

Playgrounds and Children's Behavior at Recess

Introduction

School recess, in most cases, involves outdoor play on some type of playground. In recent years, playground designs have gone through a renaissance. A drive through most towns reveals a wide array of playground structures in city parks, at daycare centers, and around public schools. An impetus for this change has come from the architecture community whose interest in design has resulted in structures that are interesting and pleasing to the eye. Further, a number of landscape architects (e.g., Moore, 1989) have involved children themselves in the design of these structures. As a social scientist, I am interested in what children do on these structures. For example, I would like to know what structures, and what aspects of these structures, are most attractive to children? What are the effects of these structures on children's behavior? In this chapter I will review the extant literature on the relation between playground design and children's behavior. For the most part, I will be examining the ways in which children act on different type of playgrounds. Hopefully, this sort of analysis will be useful to both social scientists and the landscape architects who design playgrounds.

To limit the scope of this chapter, I will not cover all aspects of children's playground behavior. I will concentrate on children's behavior on school playgrounds at recess. Other studies of outdoor play, such as anthropological (Lancy, 1984) and folklore (Sutton-Smith, 1990) studies, have been discussed elsewhere and consequently will not be reviewed here.

"Effects" of Playground Design on Playground Behavior

Educational and psychological researchers, with the exception of Frost and his colleagues (Frost & Sunderlin, 1985), have tended to ignore children's playground behaviors. Scholars from other fields, however, have spent considerable time describing children's behavior on playgrounds, both in and out of school. As noted above, landscape architects (e.g., Moore, 1988), environmental psychologists (e.g., Hayward, Rothenberg, & Beasley, 1974), and developmental psychologists (e.g., Sluckin, 1981) have provided excellent descriptions of the forms of play children exhibit on different types of school playgrounds. This work generally has described children's playground preferences and the relations between types of playground design and forms of children's behavior. Because this work has been reviewed elsewhere (Frost, 1986), I will discuss only briefly the main findings reported by other researchers. I will, however, point out some limitations in this work and indicate directions for future research.

One of the first studies of children's playground behavior was conducted by a group of environmental psychologists (Hayward et al., 1974). This was the pioneering study in the field, even though it examined neighborhood, not school, playgrounds. In this report three types of playground environments were compared: traditional, contemporary, and adventure playgrounds. Traditional playgrounds are probably most familiar to us; they consist of fixed structures, such as swings, seesaws, and jungle gyms, standing on asphalt surfaces. Contemporary playgrounds are aesthetically pleasing to look at (to adults at least), for they are often designed by architects. They are typically composed of stone, culverts, railroad ties, and the like. Adventure playgrounds are composed of a variety of materials that children can use to build their own play environments. Not surprisingly, Hayward and colleagues found different playground types were related to different play behaviors.

Generally, traditional playgrounds were attended by children least frequently and were the least likely to sustain play. Haywood and colleagues suggested that the functional diversity of adventure and contemporary playgrounds was responsible for their popularity with children and for their ability to sustain play. This finding was replicated by Naylor (1985) in the United Kingdom. These studies, through interesting and pioneering, have several important limitations. The first and most obvious limitations is self-selection. That is, different types of children may have chosen to go to specific playgrounds. If so, differences in the behaviors exhibited on each of the playgrounds could reflect differences in the personalities of the children who chose to play at those specific playgrounds. Moreover, different types of playgrounds tend to be built in different neighborhoods; consequently, the behaviors children exhibit on playgrounds are also influenced by socioeconomic and personality variables.

A second and related limitation of these free-selection public playground studies derives from the age differences of children observed on the different playgrounds. More specifically, in the Hayward et al. study, the percentage of preschool-age children observed on traditional, contemporary, and adventure playgrounds was 29.5, 25.2, and 1.8 percent, respectively; while the percentage of schoolage children on these different types of playgrounds was 20.8, 22.2, and 44.6 percent, respectively (Hayward et al., 1974). Observed behavior differences on the three playgrounds, then, may have been due to the age of the children, the type of playground, or the interaction between age and playground type. But these limitations should in no way devalue the importance of this work. It was pioneering in the early 1970s for social scientists to study children on playgrounds. Further, the descriptive information concerning children attending neighborhood playgrounds is certainly valuable in and of itself. As descriptive data, however, they do not inform us as to the "effects" of playground designs on children's behavior.

Some of these limitations can be and have been remediated by observing children's behavior in other naturalistic settings: playgrounds during school recess periods. The self-selection and differential age effects are controlled in these "natural experiments" because all children of a particular, often uniform, age range are required, weather permitting, to be on the playground for the daily recess period. Important work in this area has been conducted by Frost and colleagues (e.g., Frost, 1986; Frost & Sunderlin, 1985).

These researchers have examined the behavior of preschool and elementary school children on different playgrounds. The specific aspects of behavior they examined were the social and cognitive dimensions of children's play as defined by Parten (1932) and Smilansky (1968), respectively. The social dimensions of play are based on the seminal work of Parten (1932) who suggested that children's social participation went through the following stages: solitary (playing alone), parallel (playing next to but not with another child), associative (playing with others in a group whose composition changes frequently), and cooperative (sustained interactive playing).

The cognitive dimensions of play are based on the work of Smilansky (1968). She, like Parten, posited a hierarchy of play forms. The behaviors in the cognitive model include functional play (repetitious actions), constructive play (making things), dramatic play (make-believe), and playing games with rules.

Using these separate cognitive and social dimensions of behavior, Frost (1986) examined the effects of different types of playgrounds (i.e., traditional, contemporary, adventure, and creative) on preschool and elementary school children's play. His results suggest that functional play characterized play on traditional playgrounds while dramatic play occurred on creative playgrounds. Children tended to engage in cooperative interaction on all playgrounds.

While this body of research provides interesting data on the relations between types of playgrounds and children's behavior, questions arise from the ways in which children's play was categorized. At one level there are problems with using the hierarchical categories of Parten and Smilansky in the observational model used by Frost. Moreover, factors other than playground type influence children's playground behavior. Each of these issues will be discussed separately.

Issues Related to Observational Categories

The first issue involving the categorization system used, that is, the Parten-Smilansky model, relates to its construct validity. The hierarchical nature of each model has been questioned. Specifically, Bakeman and Brownlee (1980) have suggested that parallel interaction is not a stage but instead a strategy that children use. That is, children of various ages often establish physical proximity to others as a strategy to enter a group; it is not a stage that is distinct to any one group. Another validity-related issue concerning Parten's categories relates to the difficulty of reliably differentiating associative from cooperative interaction (Rubin, Fein, & Vandenberg, 1983). Because researchers have had difficulty differentiating the two forms of social interaction, collapsing the two categories into a social interactive category is recommended (Rubin et al., 1983). As reliability is necessary, but not sufficient, for validity, this seems to be another validity problem with the Parten model as used by Frost.

Regarding Smilansky's model, the notion that construction is play per se is doubtful. Piaget's (1970) theory of play, on which Smilansky based her model, did not consider constructive activity to be play; he considered it predominantly accommodative, not assimilative. In support of this claim, constructive activity does not follow the inverted-U developmental function that other aspects of play follow (Smith, Takhvar, Gore, & Vollstedt, 1986). Thus, there are also construct validity problems with the cognitive dimensions of the model.

A further limitation with the Parten-Smilansky model is evidenced when the model is used with schoolage children. Both of these models were designed primarily to describe the play of preschool, not primary school, children. More specifically, Parten was concerned with the processes by which preschool children moved from solitary to social interaction, while Smilansky was concerned with the movement from functional play to games with rules; only games with rules continue to increase in frequency and complexity during the elementary school years. In short, there is a mismatch between the observational model and the age of the children observed.

The problems inherent in this mismatch become clear when we consider what both preschool and elementary school children do on playgrounds. Almost 15 percent (Humphreys & Smith, 1984; see Chapter 6) of their behavior is rough-and-tumble play, a playful behavior which is not accounted for in the Parten-Smilansky model. Further, aggression cannot be accounted for by this model.

Thus, the use of this model results in an observational system that is not exhaustive, that is, the model does not account for all, or even most, of children's playground behaviors. An exhaustive criterion is necessary if we are to understand children's behavior in a particular context (Bakeman & Gottman, 1986). Such omissions are also important from a functional perspective; that is, these omitted behaviors, as will be illustrated below, have important implications for children's social cognitive development.

To remedy this problem, I recommend that observers of children's playground behavior construct "behavioral inventories" or ethograms for children of different ages. This work has been done for English preschool (Blurton Jones, 1972, 1976) and elementary school children (Humphreys & Smith, 1984). This approach, which follows an ethological model, initially describes children's behaviors at a microlevel (e.g., clenched-hand beat). These microbehaviors become the basis for more inclusive, macrolevel categories (e.g., clenched-hand beat is part of a category called aggression). This ethological approach results in behavioral categories that are age- and context-appropriate, as well as categories that are exhaustive and mutually exclusive. While there are inherent problems with basing categories on discrete bits of behavior, rather than sequences of behavior, this method is at least a starting point in inventorying children's behavior on playgrounds.

Other Factors Affecting Behavior: Environmental Variables

The studies reviewed above make implicit or explicit causal statements about relations between the playground environment and children's behaviors. As a qualifier, I do not denigrate descriptive studies. Indeed, we need more of them in this area. Correspondingly, researchers should not make cause-effect statements when they are not merited by the design of the study.

To my knowledge, only one study (Hart & Sheehan, 1986) is capable of making a causal statement about the "effects" of playgrounds on behavior because in this study children were randomly assigned to environments. Hart and Sheehan's results, unlike the findings of Frost (1986) and his colleagues, suggest that preschool children exhibit more advanced behavior on *traditional* playgrounds rather than on contemporary playgrounds. The contrasting results of Frost and Hart and Sheehan may be due to the fact that these non-randomized studies confounded playground type with other variables; for example, there may be systematic differences between the schools that choose to have different types of playgrounds. The results of Hart and Sheehan should be replicated, however, before too much confidence is put in them.

The generalizability of the results of *all* comparative playground studies should be interpreted cautiously. The differences in children's behavior in different studies may be due as much to *within*-playground variation as to *across*-playground variation. Children act differently on different parts of contemporary playgrounds (see Chapter 4) and on different parts of traditional playgrounds (Humphreys & Smith, 1984; Naylor, 1985). As a result, playgrounds with different subcomponents, even though they fall within one general type (e.g., contemporary), will elicit different types of behavior. For example, Naylor (1985) found that children talked more while playing on swings than while playing on slides. Further, elementary school children's rough-and-tumble (R&T) play occurs more frequently on soft, grassy areas than on the hard-top areas of traditional (Humphreys & Smith, 1984) and contemporary playgrounds (see Chapter 4). The results illustrate that there is great within-playground variation. Consequently, we should interpret results from different studies with different playground components cautiously. Future research should address specifically the extent to which playground components (e.g., slides) affect behavior.

Thus far I have reviewed studies concerned with the effects of specific environments or contexts on children's behavior. The contextual variables examined have been related to dimensions of the playground. Other dimensions of the physical context also seem to affect children's behavior. These other environmental dimensions of the physical environment of the playground include weather, time of day, and length of play period.

The impact of weather on playground behavior is obvious. In extreme environments (e.g., very hot or very cold) children spend less time playing than they do in more temperate environments (Naylor, 1985). Within a temperate environment, schoolchildren at recess seem to engage in more exercise play (e.g., running, chasing, and climbing) on sunny, warm days than on cold, rainy days (Smith & Hagan, 1980).

The effect of time of day and recess duration on playground behavior has been examined in only two studies, to my knowledge; these were reviewed in Chapter 1. This discussion of environmental effects on children's play should cause researchers to question the generalizability of individual studies. Even when children are randomly assigned to specific playgrounds, factors such as time of previous confinement and individual playground components affect children's playground behavior.

Possible Functions of Children's Playground Behavior

In this section the functional significance of children's playground behavior will be briefly reviewed; more thorough coverage is provided in Chapters 6, 7, 9, and 10. Functional significance is defined in a broad sense wherein a behavior has beneficial consequences on other things (Hinde, 1982). From a theoretical perspective, this issue provides insight into the role of play in children's development. That is, what are the consequences of certain behaviors for children? From an applied, or educational, perspective, it tells us about developmental/learning opportunities on the playground.

While the theoretical models describing the role of play in development typically describe the role of play in preschool children's cognitive development (e.g., Piaget, 1970; Vygotsky, 1967), the models for explaining children's outdoor behavior typically are based on animal models and relate play to children's social development (e.g., Blurton Jones, 1972; Fagen, 1981; Smith & Connolly, 1972). The method used by both groups to explicate the role of play in development typically has been to correlate measures of play with contemporaneous and longitudinal measures of children's competence (Rubin, 1982; Rubin & Daniels-Beirness, 1983; Smith & Lewis, 1985). Longitudinal studies in most areas of children's play, it should be noted, are rare. As such, the question of the developmental function of play is still unclear. The studies presented here do not, then, directly and fully address this functional question.

The cross-sectional relations between measures of outdoor play and social competence discussed here should be tested in longitudinal research designs. As a starting point, we have good theory to suggest a functional relation between various forms of playground behavior and social competence (see Fagen, 1981). By "social competence" I mean children's engagement with the environment; this construct has cognitive and social dimensions (Waters & Sroufe, 1983). For example, kindergarten children's ability to enter a play group successfully would be a measure of social competence.

Generally, theory and exploratory data suggest that some forms of social behavior observed on the playground, like R & T and other forms of reciprocal interaction, serve social skills training and practice functions for elementary school children (Humphreys & Smith, 1984; Pellegrini, 1987; also see Chapters 7 and 10). It is argued that through these behaviors children form and practice a number of social skills that are necessary for social competence. For example, in all forms of reciprocal social interaction, children alternate and negotiate roles (e.g., chaser/chased). This activity relates to children having a repertoire of social problem-solving strategies and engaging in rule-governed social games (Pellegrini, 1987).

The limited work done in this area supports these theoretical claims. More specifically, there is a significant positive relation between preschoolers' R&T and sociometric status (Smith & Lewis, 1985). At the elementary school level, these relations continue to hold, particularly for boys (see Chapter 7). Further, children, though not adolescents, who engage in R&T do so with children of similar sociometric and dominance status (Humphreys & Smith, 1986). This suggest that R&T is a friendly endeavor in which closely matched children try out and learn new social skills.

Another social skill, social problem solving as measured by children providing a variety of solutions to hypothetical social problems (Spivak & Shure, 1979), is positively related to the frequency of elementary school boys' R&T (see Chapter 6). In this form of outdoor play boys practice and/or learn to be flexible by managing roles and renegotiating rules. These behaviors are related to their more general social problem-solving skills. It has been suggested that the role alternation dimension of R&T (e.g., alternating between chaser and chased) may be responsible for improved social skills. This position is supported by other play research wherein role alternation experiences in preschoolers' dramatic play leads to improved social-cognitive status (Shantz, 1983). It is probably the case that reciprocal social interaction is an important social skills learning context.

Generally, we find that elementary school girls' playground behavior does not relate to their social competence (see Chapters 4 and 7). This is probably because the playground is a male-preferred context (Harper & Sanders, 1975), that is, given free choice, boys, more frequently than girls, will choose to go outdoors to play. As a result, girls are neither reinforced by peers or adults nor do they have models for exhibiting competence in that context. In other words, girls do not participate fully in the playground context and, as a result, we have a floor effect for girls' behavior on the playground. For this reason their playground behavior does not relate to other measures of competence. In keeping with this sex role stereotype argument, girls who do exhibit typically male behavior (e.g., R&T) on the playground are considered to be antisocial by teachers (see Chapters 4). Girls do, however, use play (e.g., dramatic play) to practice and/or develop their social cognition.

These gender differences in playground behavior and their differential correlations are an interesting illustration of the ways in which different children take different routes to some developmental milepost, such as social competence. While many, but certainly not all, boys engage in vigorous forms of reciprocal social interaction, like R&T, girls more frequently engage in social sedentary, reciprocal interaction. In the end, most of these children become competent in their own right, but they have reached this point via different routes. This notion of different routes to a specific outcome has been referred to as "equifinality" (Bertalanffy, 1952).

The results presented in this section suggest that the playground does provide opportunities for some children, especially male children, to learn or develop social skills. As such, it should be treated as an environment with educational opportunities. Much more research is needed to explicate the nature and extent of these opportunities.

References

Bakeman, R., & Brownlee, J. (1980). The strategic use of parallel play: A sequential analysis: *Child Development, 51*, 873-878.

Bakeman, R., & Gottman, J. (1986). *Observing interaction: An introduction to sequential analysis*. New York: Cambridge University Press.

Bertalanffy, L. von (1952). *Problems of life*. New York: Braziller.

Blurton Jones, N. (1972). Categories of child interaction. In N. Blurton Jones (ed.), *Ethological studies of child behavior* (pp. 97-129). London: Cambridge University Press.

———. (1976). Rough-and tumble play among nursery school children. In J. Bruner, A. Jolly, & K. Sylva (eds.), *Play—Its role in development and evolution* (pp. 352-363). New York: Basic Books.

DeStefano, J. (1984). Learning to communicate in the classroom. In A. Pellegrini & T. Yawkey (eds.), *The development of oral and written language in social context* (pp. 155-166). Norwood, NJ: Ablex.

Dodge, K., & Frame, C. (1982). Social cognitive biases and deficits in aggressive boys. *Child Development, 53*, 620-635.

Frost, J. (1986). Children's playgrounds: Research and practice. In G. Fein & M. Rivkin (eds.), *The young child at play: Reviews of research* (Vol. 4, pp. 195-212).

Washington, DC: National Association for the Education of Young Children.

Frost, J., & Sunderlin, S. (Eds.). (1985). *When children play*. Wheaton, MD: Association for Childhood Education International.

Glickman, C. (1984). Play in public school settings: A philosophical question. In A. Pellegrini & T. Yawkey (eds.), *Child's play* (pp. 255-272). Hillside, NJ: Erlbaum.

Groos, K. (1898). *The play of animals*. New York: Appleton.

Harper, L., & Sanders, K. (1975). Preschool children's use of space: Sex differences in outdoor play. *Developmental Psychology, 11*, 119.

Hart, C., & Sheehan, R. (1986). Preschoolers' play behavior in outdoor environments: Effects of traditional and contemporary playgrounds. *American Educational Research Journal, 23*, 669-679.

Hartup, W. (1983). Peer relations. In E. M. Hetherington (ed.), *Handbook of child psychology* (Vol. 4, pp. 103-196). New York: Wiley.

Hayward, G., Rothenberg, M., & Beasley, R. (1974). Children's play and urban playground environments: A comparison of traditional contemporary, and adventure types. *Environment and Behavior, 6*, 131-168.

Henninger, M. (1985). Preschool children's play behavior in indoor and outdoor environment. In J. Frost & S. Sunderlin (eds.), *When children play* (pp. 145-294). Wheaton, MD: Association for Childhood Education International.

Hinde, R. (1982). *Ethology*. London: Fontana.

Humphreys, A., & Smith, P. K. (1984). Rough-and-tumble in preschool and playground. In P. Smith (ed.), *Play in animals and humans* (pp. 241-270). Oxford: Blackwell.

————. (1987). Rough-and-tumble play, friendship and dominance in school children: Evidence for continuity and change with age. *Child Development, 58,* 201-212.

Ladd, G. (1983). Social networks of popular, average, and rejected children in school settings. *Merrill-Palmer Quarterly, 29,* 283-307.

Lancy, D. (1984). Play in anthropological perspective. In P. K. Smith (ed.), *Play in animals and humans* (pp. 295-304). Oxford: Blackwell.

Maccoby, E. (1986). Social groupings in childhood: Their relationship to prosocial and antisocial behavior in boys and girls. In D. Olweus, J. Block, & M. Radye-Yarrow (eds.), *Development of antisocial and prosocial behavior: Research, theory and issues* (pp. 263-284). New York: Academic Press.

Maccoby, E., & Jacklin, C. (1974). *The psychology of sex differences.* Stanford, CA: Stanford University Press.

Marchessault, K., McAffer, V., & Servin, L. (1987, April). *Social initiation on the playground: A naturalistic study of withdrawn children.* Poster session at the bienniel meeting of the Society for Research in Child Development, Baltimore.

Money, J., & Ehrhardt, A. (1972). *Man and woman, boy and girl.* Baltimore: Johns Hopkins University Press.

Moore, R. (1989). Before and after asphalt: Diversity as an ecological measure of quality of children's outdoor environments. In M. Bloch & A. Pellegrini (eds.), *The ecological context of children's play* (pp. 191-213). Norwood, NJ: Ablex.

Naylor, H. (1983). Design for outdoor play: An observational study. In J. Frost & S. Sunderlin (eds.), *When children play* (pp. 103-113). Wheaton, MD: Association for Childhood Education International.

————. (1985). Outdoor play and play equipment. *Early Child Development and Care, 19* (1, 2), 109-130.

Parten, M. (1932). Social participation among preschool children. *Journal of Abnormal and Social Psychology, 27,* 243-269.

Pellegrini, A. (1987). Rough-and-tumble play: Developmental and educational significance. *Educational Psychologist, 22,* 23-43.

Piaget, J. (1970). Piaget's theory. In P. Mussen (ed.), *Carmichael's manual of child psychology* (Vol. 1, pp. 703-732). New York: Wiley.

Rubin, K. (1982). Nonsocial play in preschoolers: Necessary evil? *Child Development, 53,* 651-657.

Rubin, K., & Daniels-Beirness, T. (1983). Concurrent and predictive correlates of sociometric status in kindergarten and grade 1 children. *Merrill-Palmer Quarterly, 29,* 337-351.

Rubin, K., Fein, G., & Vandenberg, B. (1983). Play. In E. M. Hetherington (ed.), *Handbook of child psychology, socialization, personality and social development* (Vol. 4, pp. 693-774). New York: Wiley.

Serbin, L., Marchessault, K., Lyons, J., & Schwartzman, A. (1987, April). *Social behavior on the elementary school playground: An observational study of normal and atypical boys and girls.* Poster session at the bienniel meetings of the Society for Research in Child Development, Baltimore.

Shantz, C. U. (1983). Social cognition. In J. Flavell & E. Markman (eds.), *Handbook of child psychology:* vol. 3, *Cognitive development* (pp. 495-555). New York: Wiley.

Sluckin, A. (1981). *Growing up on the playground.* London: Routledge and Kegan Paul.

Smilansky, S. (1968). *The effects of sociodramatic play on disadvantaged preschool children.* New York: Wiley.

Smith, P. K. (1973). Temporal clusters and individual differences in the behavior of preschool children. In R. Michael & J. Crook (eds.), *Comparative ecology and the behavior of primates* (pp. 752-798). London: Academic Press.

Smith, P. K., & Connolly, K. (1972). Patterns of play and social interaction in pre-school children. In N. Blurton Jones (ed.), *Ethological studies in child behaviour* (pp. 65-96). London: Cambridge University Press.

———— . (1980). *The ecology of preschool behavior.* London: Cambridge University Press.

Smith, P. K., & Hagan, T. (1980). Effects of deprivation on exercise play in nursery school children. *Animal Behaviour, 28,* 922-928.

Smith, P. K., & Lewis, K. (1985). Rough-and-tumble play, fighting, and chasing in nursery school children. *Ethology and Sociobiology, 6,* 175-181.

Smith, P. K., Takhar, M., Gore, N., & Vollstedt, R. (1986). Play in young children: Problems of definition, categorization, and measurement. *Early Child Development and Care, 19* (1, 2), 25-42.

Spivak, G., & Shure, M. (1979). *Social adjustment of young children*. San Francisco: Jossey-Bass.

Vygotsky, L. (1967). Play and its role in the mental development of the child. *Soviet Psychology, 12*, 62-76.

Waters, E., & Stroufe, L. (1983). Social competence as a developmental construct. *Developmental Review, 3*, 79-97.

3

Theory and Method

An Autobiographical Narrative

I came to the study of children on the playground rather indirectly. I say "indirectly" because when I started this venture I had no intent of spending nearly 10 years on it.

My graduate training and early career were centered around children's symbolic play and their accompanying oral language. Following the excellent traditions in this field I was guided by models in developmental, psychology, cognitive psychology, and sociolinguistics. This path led me, as it has many others, to an interest in the nature of development per se and to the ways in which children's transactions with their environments defined individual development. Specifically, I was led to the work of the English human ethologists, particularly Peter K. Smith, Kevin Connolly, William McGrew, Nick Blurton Jones, and Robert Hinde. The work of these scholars was particularly attractive to me in that it proposed, in testable terms, specific ways by which children's development was determined by their interaction in different ecologies. I was determined to learn more about this topic. To this end, I went to Sheffield University in 1984 to work with two pioneers in the field, Peter K. Smith and Kevin Connolly. At the time Smith was working on one aspect of children's play behavior, rough-and-tumble play (R&T). I undertook the study of R&T, so I thought, simply as a way by which to learn ethological methods. My reasoning was as follows: I know about play but I don't know about ethology, therefore ethological studies of play in the form of R&T would be a good way of bridging the gap. So, upon returning to the United States, tape recorder in hand, I started frequenting playgrounds at recess. Nine years and another visit to Sheffield later, I still frequent playgrounds, tape recorder in hand.

So much for autobiographical narrative. In the remainder of this chapter I outline the assumptions that guided this research program. This entails outlining some of the assumptions of the ethological method, generally, and of the observational methodology. Such an explication is necessary to the extent that the theory and methods are both important dimensions of this work. While other research methods, such as ethnography (e.g., Finnan, 1982; Sluckin, 1981), have been applied to the playground, they will not be reviewed here for they were not used in the work discussed in this volume. Next, I will address the observational methods, procedures, and logistics in the studies discussed in this volume.

Ethological Methods

Ethology has its intellectual roots in the biological study of behavior (Cairns, 1986; Martin & Bateson, 1986) and is biased toward examining children, at least initially, in their natural environments. This bias toward studying behavior and development in natural environments reflects the Darwinian origins of ethology. Specifically, ethologists believe that organisms' behaviors and development are a result of their transactions with and adaptations to the environment. Detailed descriptions, or ethograms, are the exhaustive behavioral inventories that ethologists construct in the descriptions of animals in their environments. As we will see later, the ways in which the behaviors are described and categorized are different and reflect interesting theoretical orientations.

Describing and Categorizing Behavior

The enterprise of describing and categorizing behavior presents an interesting theoretical and methodological problem. In attempting to describe behavior a number of important choices must be made because, especially when we are observing humans, there are simply too many things to observe. Thus choices about inclusion and exclusion must be made; we simply cannot describe everything. Consequently, deciding what to observe and what to ignore are theoretical choices, whether they are made implicitly or explicitly. That is, by extracting certain behaviors from their social and physical environments we are making decisions about what is important and what is not important. This act of extracting and categorizing behaviors, as Robert Hinde (1992) reminds us, is destroying nature.

Two Ways of Describing Behavior

I will begin this subsection with an excerpt from one of my favorite naturalists, Beatrix Potter.

This is a fierce bad Rabbit; look at his savage whiskers, and his claws and his turned-up tail.

This is a nice gentle Rabbit. His mother has given him a carrot.

The bad rabbit would like some carrot.

He doesn't say "Please." He takes it!

And he scratches the good Rabbit very badly.

The good Rabbit creeps away, and hides in a hole. It feels sad. (Potter, 1989, pp. 133-135)

As Ms Potter shows us, behavior can, generally, be described in two ways. The first involves describing individual motor patterns, such as "turned up tail," "claws," and "scratches." Applied to children in the playground, such descriptions could include "hit at with open hand." Other forms of description include describing the consequences of specific behaviors; the good rabbit creeping away following the "scratching" is such an example. Applied to children in the playground, "hit at with open hands followed by smile" and "leaving the scene" are illustrative. In both cases the act of categorization assigns meaning to the behaviors in question. The rabbits are either bad or good depending on the behaviors described or by the consequences of their actions.

In the first case, meaning is assigned to individual motor patterns by association; that is, the meaning of one behavior is determined by the other behaviors with which it co-occurs. These groups of co-occurring behavior form categories. For example, "hit at with open hand" may co-occur with other behaviors, such as "smile," "run," and "grapple"; we could label this group of behavior "rough play." Factor analysis techniques are typically used to determine the extent to which behaviors co-occur empirically.

Relatedly, we could look at the consequences of "hit at with open hand" and find that it is followed by" "run," "hug," and "chase." We could label this category "rough play" because it is physically rough yet leads to reciprocal role taking. Obviously, these two methods of category induction are not independent of each other: individual behaviors that co-occur may also co-occur in antecedent-consequence order. The benefit of description by consequence is that it does not examine behaviors in isolation from each other. It makes an attempt to keep them embedded in the sequence in which they occur in nature. This route also allows us to come closer to understanding the function, or meaning, behind behaviors. That is, by looking at the consequences of behavior we can make come closer to understanding the ways in which the participants encountered them, and consequently we come closer to making accurate assumptions about the meaning of behaviors than if we only were to describe individual behaviors. For example, by noting that "hit at with open hand" has the consequence of being "hugged" by another child, we can assume that the motivation for exhibiting the first behavior was to elicit the second; thus, we can say that the "hit at with open hand" is an affiliative behavior. When working with children, at least children old enough to talk with us, we have the added benefit of being able to ask them what certain behaviors mean; thus we can check our interpretations by directly asking children or other participants, such as teachers.

Describing Rough Play: Co-occurrence

In the remainder of this section, I will review ethological studies of children's play, of which rough play was a reliable component. The early studies described all relied on behavioral co-occurrence of behaviors to induce categories; later studies looked at consequences of behavior as well. All these studies relied on behavior descriptions for categorization. Next I will describe other research wherein we asked children to describe their own and others' rough play.

During the 1970s a group of ethologists applied their methods of studying animals to studying children's behavior generally, including their play. These scholars, in good ethological tradition, relied on microanalytical behavioral descriptions to categorize children's play. These early efforts were generally limited to the study of preschool children; that is, children between two and five years old.

Peter Smith and Kevin Connolly's work was published initially along with that of Nicholas Blurton Jones in 1972. The aim of these early papers was to generate *ethograms*, or detailed behavioral inventories, of children in preschool classrooms and on playgrounds. Smith and Connolly (1972) observed children (M = 45 months old) in their preschool classrooms using focal child sampling and instantaneous recording rules (these terms are defined later in this chapter). Individual behaviors were factor analyzed and three categories were identified: social maturity (talks to other children, group play, and age were positive dimensions, while stares and self-behavior were negative dimensions), plays with/without toys, and cry/distress.

Blurton Jones's (1972) study, reported in the same volume, with children 2- to 4-years-old, utilized focal child sampling and continuous recording techniques and derived very similar categories to those of Smith and Connolly (1972). A factor similar to the social maturity factor emerged with plays with others, smiles, and talks on the positive side, and crys, passive, watches others on the negative side. A second play factor was also identified with R&T and play with toys as components. Unlike Smith and Connolly (1972), however, Blurton Jones found an aggression factor, composed of fixate, frown, and take. Interesting from our perspective was the fact that aggression and R&T did not co-occur. That is, R&T did not seem to have an aggressive component. A subsequent study by Smith (1973) replicated the factor structures found in the earlier two investigations. Thus, children's behavior in their preschool classrooms could be reliably placed into three categories, one of which was a play category and independent of aggression.

In a later study of preschool children (M = 48 months old) in their preschool class and playground, Roper and Hinde (1978) used scan sampling and instantaneous recording rules to categorize behavior. Their results, however, differed from those reported above. Only a social maturity factor was in common with the earlier research. Solitary play and social immaturity factors emerged in the Roper and Hinde study but were not evident in the other work. The lack of concordance between the last study and the preceding two studies may have been due to the contexts in which the different studies took place. Specifically, there seemed to be important differences between the classrooms in which the children were observed. Indeed, Roper and Hinde suggested that the "nature" of their classrooms may have ruled out the possibility of a playing with/without toy factor emerging.

While they offer no further details regarding this explanation, one can easily come up with a number of candidates. School policy, for example, often discourages certain types of play, such as R&T and imaginary gun play. This could easily explain differences in children exhibiting specific forms of play.

Another relevant classroom factor is classroom size. Roper and Hinde's classrooms were described as large and well equipped; children were also observed in the playground. While no outdoor play was observed by Smith (1973), the classrooms he observed were large (400-500 square feet per child) and contained toys similar to those mentioned by Roper and Hinde. The social density in the Blurton Jones (1972) and Smith and Connolly (1972) studies, however, were very different. I calculated about 25 square feet per child in the former study and about 65 square feet per child in the latter study; both study areas were equipped with similar toys. Thus,

Roper and Hinde may have observed unoccupied and solitary behavior because children were observed in spacious settings. Of course that does not explain the difference between this study and Smith's (1973). It may be the case that the nonsocial behavior described by Roper and Hinde tended to occur outdoors, a context not observed by Smith (1973). Without better behavior × context descriptions, this cannot be empirically determined. Thus, it becomes important for observers to document the ways in which behaviors vary according to different social and physical contexts. Indeed, a crucial dimension of ethological theory involves documenting this relationship. Behaviors and environments interact with each other: we cannot understand one without the other.

Describing Rough Play: Consequences

Behavior can also be categorized according to consequences. To do so, however, requires a specific observational technique. If we are interested in describing the extent to which behaviors co-occur within a group of children we can use a variety of observational recording techniques. If we are *not* interested in specific *sequences* of behavior we can record behaviors with any of the following rules: instantaneous, 1/0, or continuous. The data provided by the first two rules are not sequential but do tell us the extent to which behaviors tend to co-occur within a group of children and within certain observational time parameters. Sequential data, like antecedent-consequence data, can only be derived from continuous recording.

In our observational studies of children's and adolescents' playground behavior continuous recording rules were used to determine the extent to which R&T bouts were followed by aggressive or affiliative behaviors. If R&T was followed by aggression we would define R&T as an aggressive and antisocial category, but if it was followed by affiliative behaviors it would be defined as affiliative; thus, meaning is derived from the consequences of behavior.

Among primary school-age children we find that R&T on the playground is generally followed by affiliative behaviors, such as reciprocal games. Again, the data must be qualified by noting that context has an interactive effect. In this case, the context involved and the type of children exhibiting the R&T bouts both determine the meaning of the behavior. If the children are rejected by their peers and have a history of aggressive behavior, R&T will not move into other forms of playful and affiliative behavior. Instead it will "escalate" into aggression. For other, nonaggressive, children, however, R&T is reliably followed by affiliative behavior. Thus, for most primary school children

R&T, from a consequential perspective, can be defined as an affiliative and playful category (see Chapters 7 and 10).

The meaning of a behavior, or a set of behaviors, also varies according to the age of the child exhibiting it or them. The cry of an infant means one thing, whereas the cry of an adolescent probably means something very different. So too with various social behaviors, like R&T. Whereas the R&T for most primary school children is affiliative and playful, we find that during early adolescence it is generally aggressive and used to exhibit dominance (see Chapters 7 and 10).

Describing Rough Play: Interview Techniques

The methods used to infer category membership and meaning described in the preceding section were derived from researchers studying nonhuman animals. Consequently, researchers could not ask their research subjects what a specific behavior means or what category it belongs to! While this can be done with children, it often does not provide a clear-cut answer. There are numerous, well-documented problems with interview and introspective data, such as reactivity. These problems are compounded when interviewing children, who often assign different meanings to words than do the interviewers. The construct of "intersubjectivity" has been used to describe the processes by which interactants jointly construct and exchange meaning. (See Garvey, in press, for a play-related discussion.) Thus, caution must be exercised in interpreting both interview and behavioral data. The best way to proceed may be to treat interview and behavioral data as complementary, that is, we must ask To what extent do they tell us the same thing? If they do not converge, we should exercise more caution than in cases of convergence. Ethnogrpahers too use these techniques by determining the extent to which interview data "triangulate" with other data sources, such as observations and artifacts.

When preschool and primary school children are asked to differentiate between R&T and aggression, they do so reliably (see Chapter 7). That is, when nonaggressive children view videotapes of other children engaging in R&T or aggression they can discriminate between R&T and aggression at beyond chance levels. Thus, and consistent with the behavioral record, most children see R&T and aggression as separate categories of behavior. The ways in which aggressive children respond to interviews is also consistent with their behavior. They do not tend to differentiate R&T from aggression.

Accuracy in discriminating R&T and aggression is also affected by more immediate factors. Specifically, children viewing videotapes of R&T and aggressive bouts in which *they participated* are more accurate in discriminating between R&T and aggression even one week after the actual behaviors were recorded, than are nonparticipants (Smees, 1992). The nonparticipants in this case were either teachers or classmates of the taped children. Thus, and not surprisingly, participation in an event leads to a more accurate perception of that event than nonparticipation. By way of explanation of this finding, it may be the case that participants in R&T bouts are more accurate than nonparticipants because children tend to engage in R&T with friends (Humphreys & Smith, 1987). Friends, compared to nonfriends, tend to be understand behaviors among themselves. Thus, it may be that friendship status, rather than participation, is important in interpreting R&T and aggression.

There are also interesting methodological and theoretical implications for this work. That different people proffer different interpretations of events should lead to our minimizing the role of one source of data. Specifically, the above data clearly indicate that teachers, nonparticipating children, and observers often have interpretations of events that contradict the interpretations of the participants. Indeed, it may be the case that participants themselves may differ in interpretations, depending on relationships variables, like friendship. Thus, there do not seem to be "hallowed" data sources, such as teachers or children. Interviewing people who take different perspectives on an event is a valuable complement to descriptions generated via behavioral observations.

Observational Methods

Behavioral observations are an important source of information. As I noted above, interview and questionnaire methodologies, when used alone, suffered from numerous limitations. Similarly, when behavioral observations alone are used they too have limitations, though of a different sort. In this section I will outline different ways in which behavioral observations have been used to study children's playground behavior.

As I noted above, before observations actually begin researchers must make general choices as to what should be observed and what should not be observed. These issues were addressed specifically under the rubric of categorizations. That is not to say that categories are defined a priori; indeed, category systems may change after the observers actually enter the field.

Entering the Field

Preliminary observations are a necessary first step in all observational work. These preliminary sessions enable the researcher to more clearly formulate his or her research questions, determine coding categorization systems to be used, and determine the recording methods to be used (Martin & Batsoen, 1986). Specific to the research question, some firsthand knowledge is essential, especially when studying play, generally, and rough play, specifically. It may be the case, for example, that school policy, either explicitly or implicitly, prohibits specific forms of rough behavior, like play fighting. Consequently, these behaviors may not be readily observable. Only by spending time observing and talking with school personnel and students can such policy be determined. Relatedly, if one is interested in studying aggression, a behavior explicitly discouraged in most schools and consequently not easily observed, it may take both interviewing and observations in a number of contexts to determine where most observational time should be spent.

Regarding the issue of categorization, initial observations help researchers determine the specific category system that is most effectively used in a specific setting. For example, it may be the case that researchers realize, after repeated observations, that children from a specific school are particularly sensitive to observer presence. To minimize such obtrusive effects, observations must be conducted from a distance, using either binoculars or a zoom-lens videocamera. Observations from a distance, of course, preclude the use of children's verbalizations as a category. Thus, children's games in which the rules are verbally stated may not be observable. By way of remedy, children could be equiped with wireless microphones so that their language can be recorded while they are being filmed from a distance. While obtrusive at first, wireless microphones soon become second nature to most children.

Recording accurate (i.e., reliable) behavioral data involves initial, and repeated, checking of categorization systems. Initial practice observations are usually necessary until observers master the system. As it typically happens, when observers gain experience they become more expert at the system. To avoid "observer drift," an initial training period and subsequent retraining periods are necessary to maintain adequate levels of interobserver agreement.

At another level, initial observations help to sort out mechanical problems. For example, in our first observations of R&T we attempted to have observers record children's behavior continuously on a checklist. It quickly became obvious when we tried using this system that observers spent too much time looking for the codes on the checklist and not enough time actually observing behaviors. To fix this problem, observers were trained to describe behaviors into a tape recorder and then later transcribe the behaviors onto coding sheets. While this meant another time-consuming step had to be added to the process, it resulted in seemingly better data.

Familiarization is a crucial aspect of entering the field. By "familiarization" I mean that children must become familiar with the observers and vice versa. That the children feel comfortable around observers is obviously important, particularly when the behaviors of interest, such as aggression or play fighting, are explicitly or implicitly forbidden. Only by spending lots of time on the playground, interacting minimally with children, will the children habituate to their observers. By "minimally interactive" I mean that observers do not initiate interaction with children and they are minimally responsive to their demands. For example, when children asked me why I was talking into a tape recorder or what I was doing on the playground, I merely said I was interested in what kids did at recess and moved away.

It is also important that observers become familiar with the children. Observers must be able to quickly identify focal children and their playmates. This can be a very intimidating task when 75 children are running around a large play area. The way in which we handled this problem was to first take pictures of all the children. If class pictures are available they will do. Individual pictures are then mounted on 3 × 5 index cards and labeled with the child's name. Before each observation period observers spend time identifying the children they will be observing that day. Identification markers, such as the color of the children's shirt or coat for each child can be noted on small "post-it" papers and attached to the pictures. With time children are easily identified. It is particularly sensible if observers spend time learning children's names and faces during the early "habituation" period. During that period when observers are spending time around the children so that the latter can habituate to the former, observers should also be learning children's names and faces. In short, entering the field is an important part of any observational study. Time taken at this point can save much time later.

Recording and Sampling Rules

The ways in which behavioral data are to be used will determine the recording and sampling rules followed (Martin & Bateson,

1986). Recording rules refer to the rules followed in actually recording the behavior and consist of the following: continuous, 0/1, and
instantaneous. Sampling rules, on the other hand, guide the ways in
which we sample behaviors from their natural streams and include:
ad libitum, focal child, scan, and behavior. *Ad libitum* sampling is
the least systematic to the extent that observers record whatever
they choose, whenever they choose. Thus, there are no corresponding
recording rules for this form of sampling. While ad lib sampling may
be useful in the initial stages of observational research, such as the
"entering the field" stage, it has obvious limitations in terms of being
biased toward observing the most visible and immediate forms of
behavior and individuals.

Focal child sampling was used extensively in our playground
research. Focal child sampling involves choosing, in advance, individuals to be observed for a predetermined time period. Our method
was to generate separate counterbalanced lists of subjects for each
period, such as separate lists for each grade per month. Focal children would be observed in the specified order for a specific duration; in our cases we used a 3-minute duration. If focal children "dis-
appeared" while being observed for more than 30 seconds,
observations were terminated and the next child was observed. Any
of the recording rules—continuous, instantaneous, or 1/0—can be
used with focal child sampling.

Our studies utilized continuous recording; that is, children's
behavior was recorded continuously for 3 minutes into a tape
recorder. In this way we not only retained the sequential integrity of
the behaviors that occurred—that is, we knew the order of events—
but we could also maintained a real time dimension by noting time
intervals from the tape recorder. So we could determine not only if
R&T was followed by aggression or not but we could also determine
the average duration of R&T bouts. Continuous recording techniques
also yield frequency data and latency data (e.g., the time between
when someone says "Stop" and when the behavior actually stops).
With all scores (i.e., duration, frequency, and latency) we need to
know the time sampling unit. For example, that 10 R&T bouts
occurred, a frequency score, is meaningless unless we know that the
score occurred during a specified time, such as 30 minutes.

By way of contrast, 1/0 recording and instantaneous recording,
unlike continuous recording, record the occurrence/nonoccurrence
of specific behaviors during a specified duration. For example, using
1/0 recording we would note the occurrence (noted by a 1) or the
nonoccurrence (noted by a 0) of a behavior during a specified time

interval, say 3 minutes. A child would get a score of 1 if he or she engaged in 1 or more R&T bouts during that interval; thus, neither frequency nor duration scores can be derived from 1/0 recording. Instantaneous recording, on the other hand, also looks for the occurrence or nonoccurrence of specified behaviors but judgments are made at a prespecified, instantaneous, time point, such as when a buzzer goes off or every 30 seconds. Relative frequencies (i.e., relative to the total number of sampling intervals) can be derived from instantaneous sampling but it does not yield relative frequencies across time periods or duration scores.

Scan sampling was also used in our studies. Scan sampling involves rapid observation with instantaneous recording. For example, as Chapter 5 on recess behavior and confinement effects notes, all children in the classroom were scan sampled, during which observers recorded degree of attention and fidgeting, and scan sampled on the playground, during which the observers recorded level of vigorous activity. In essence, scan sampling provides us with a census of activities across time. In our studies children were scan sampled only once (in each setting/day) so as to minimize interdependent observations. Specifically, if individual scan samples are to be treated as separate samples care should be taken to assure independence of observations. This is best accomplished by separating scans by means of a reasonable duration. What is reasonable, however, is an empirical issue that has been relatively unexplored. Smith (1985), for example, recommends separating scans by 4 minutes. It may be the case that specific intervals are affected by both the age of the children being observed and the context in which they are being observed.

Behavior, or event, sampling is the final sampling rule to be discussed. Unlike the other sampling rules, with possibly the exception of ad lib sampling, behavior sampling is useful in sampling unusual or rare events, such as aggression in schools. Continuous and 1/0 recording rules are used with behavior sampling. Continuous recording can be used to describe the nature of the aggressive episodes themselves while 1/0 recording can be used to describe the extent to which these rare behaviors occur or do not occur during a specific time interval. Behavior sampling and continuous recording was used in some of our R&T work to describe the nature of R&T bouts. Initiators and targets of R&T bouts were described, and so were the behaviors characterizing their play. When behaviors not included in R&T were observed, the behavior sample end, noting the behavior which succeeded R&T.

Sequences of Behavior

Sequences of behavior, rather than behaviors isolated from their behavioral stream, can also be interesting to observe. Sequential analyses, however, can only be used on continuously recorded behavior samples. At both the practical and theoretical levels analyses of sequences can provide important information. For example, and at the practical level, the degree to which R&T leads to aggression is certainly of concern to parents, teachers, and playground supervisors. Theoretically, we can begin to make inferences about the function of a behavior by looking at its consequences; thus, the extent to which R&T serves an aggressive or prosocial function can be addressed by examining the probability of R&T bouts leading to aggression or games, respectively. Also, as I noted above, sequential data are necessary when behaviors are categorized according to consequence, compared to physical descriptions

In our work with both primary and middle school children we used sequential lag analyses as outlined by Bakeman and Gottman (1986). In this procedure transitional probabilities of one behavior leading to another specified behavior are analyzed. The extent to which these probabilities occur at a rate greater than chance is determined by converting the probabilities to z-scores. Alternately, *chi*-square analyses can be used to determine the independence of a series of behaviors (Gottman & Roy, 1990). The time scale of sequential analyses is also a concern. In most cases researchers examine behaviors that occur immediately after the target behavior. For example, given the category "parallel play," what form of play occurrs when children are no longer engaged in parallel play? Other time intervals may be more useful, however. It may be the case that retaliatory forms of aggression follow specific acts, like teasing or hitting, but the retaliation occurs within the same play period, say within 20 minutes rather than immediately. By way of guidance, researchers can either use theory as a guide or conduct several continuous observations to provide some hint as to the lag between certain sequences.

Conclusion

In this chapter I have outlined a general orientation to studying children. Based on principles derived from human ethology, we can form meaningful categories of children's behavior. The ways in which we form categories, in turn, affect the functional significance of the behavior. Importantly, it is noted that children's behavior varies significantly depending on a variety of contextual factors, such as spatial density and personal relationships, and developmental factors. For example, R&T is more likely to occur between friends than between nonfriends. Further, the function of R&T seems to change from childhood to adolescence.

References

Altmann, J. (1974). Observational study of behavior: Sampling methods. *Behavior, 49*, 227-265.

Bakeman, R., & Brownlee, J. (1980). The strategic use of parallel play: A sequential analysis. *Child Development, 51*, 873-878.

Bakeman, R., & Gottman, J. (1986). *Observing interaction.* New York: Cambridge University Press.

Bekoff, M. (1979). Quantitative studies of three areas of classical ethology: Social dominance, behavioral taxonomy, and behavioral flexibility. In B. Hazlett (ed.), *Quantitative methods in the study of animal behavior* (pp. 1-46). New York: Academic Press.

Blurton Jones, N. (1972). Categories of child interaction. In N. Burton Jones (ed.), *Ethological studies of child behavior* (pp. 97-129). London: Cambridge University Press.

Bolles, R. (1979). The functional significance of behavior. *Behavioral and Brain Sciences, 2*, 29-30.

Bookstein, F. (1986). The elements of latent variable models. In M. Lamb, A. Brown, & B. Rogoff (eds.), *Advances in developmental psychology* (Vol. 4, pp. 203-230). Hillsdale, NJ: Erlbaum.

Boulton, M. (1991). A comparison of structural and contextual features of middle school children's playful and aggressive fighting. *Ethology and Sociobiology, 12*, 119-145.

Boulton, M., & Smith, P. K. (1989). Issues in the study of children's rough-and-tumble play. In M. Bloch & A. D. Pellegrini (eds.), *The ecological context of children's play* (pp. 57-83). Norwood, NJ: Ablex.

Cairns, R. (1986). An evolutionary and developmental perspective on aggressive patterns. In C. Zahn-Waxler, E. Cummings, & R. Iannotti (eds.), *Altruism and aggression* (pp. 58-87). New York: Cambridge University Press.

Charlesworth, W. (1983). An ethological approach to cognitive development. In C. Brainerd (ed.), *Recent advances in cognitive development theory* (pp. 237-258). New York: Springer-Verlag.

Eibl-Eibesfeldt, I. (1979). Human ethology: Concepts and implications for the sciences of man. *Behavioral and Brain Sciences, 2,* 1-57.

Finnan, C. (1982). The ethnography of children's play. In G. Spindler (ed.), *Doing the ethnography of schooling* (pp. 356-380). New York: Holt, Rinehart and Winston.

Fry, D. (1987). Differences between play fighting and serious fights among Zaotec children. *Ethology and Sociobiology, 8,* 285-306.

Garvey, C. (1984). *Children's talk.* Cambridge, MA: Harvard University Press.

————. (in press). Intersubjectivity and framing in pretend play interactions. *Human Development.*

Gottlieb, G. (1983). The psychobiological approach to developmental issues. In J. J. Campos & M. H. Haith (eds.), *Handbook of child psychology: Infancy and developmental psychobiology* (Vol. 2, pp. 1-26). New York: Wiley.

Gottman, J., & Roy, A. (1990). *Sequential analysis.* New York: Cambridge University Press.

Hinde, R. (1983). Ethology and child development. In J. J.Campos & M. H. Haith (eds.), *Handbook of child psychology: Infancy and developmental psychobiology* (Vol. 2, pp. 27-99). New York: Wiley.

————. (1992). *Individuals, relationships, and culture.* New York: Cambridge University Press.

Lykken, D. (1968). Statistical significance in psychological research. *Psychological Bulletin, 70,* 151-159.

Martin, P., & Bateson, P. (1986). *Measuring behavior.* London: Cambridge University Press.

McGrew, W. (1972). *An ethological study of children's behavior.* London: Metheun.

Potter, B. (1989). The Story of the Fierce Bad Rabbit. In *The Complete Tales of Beatrix Potter* (pp. 131-138). London: Warne.

Roper, R., & Hinde, R. (1978). Social play in a play group: Consistency and complexity. *Child Development, 49,* 570-579.

Sluckin, A. (1981). *Growing up in the playground*. London: Routledge and Kegan Paul.

Smees, R. (1992). *An investigation into the effects of participation and non-participation on the perceptions of playfighting and real fighting*. Unpublished B.A. Dissertation. Sheffield University, Sheffield, UK.

Smith, P. K. (1973). Temporal clusters and individual differences in the behavior of preschool children. In R. Michael & J. Crook (eds.), *Comparative ecology and behavior*. London: Academic Press.

———. (1985). The reliability and validity of one-zero sampling. *British Educational Research Journal, 11*, 215-220.

4

Dimensions of the Playground and Children's Behavior: Implications for Social Cognition Development

Introduction

In the preceding chapter I reviewed the ways in which the different dimensions of playgrounds related to children's behavior. Recall that in many of the studies I reviewed, children's playground behavior was coded according to some variation of the Smilansky (1968) and/or Parten (1932) systems. It was noted that these systems are appropriate for studying the classroom play behavior of preschool children but less appropriate for studying primary school children on the playground. Briefly, most categories in those systems are skewed toward younger children; for example, three out of the four Smilansky categories are typical of preschool children's play. Further, the categories, even for preschool children, do not account for many behaviors that occur on the playground, such as rough-and-tumble play and aggression.

The behavioral measures used for data discussed in this chapter were the result of ethological observations of primary school children's playground behaviors. As I noted in Chapter 3, ethological methods involve creating categories based on the specific behaviors children exhibit in specific circumstances. Consequently, inductive category systems are used. This practice is indicative of the theoretical bias in ethology according to which behaviors and context can only be understood in relation to each other. This is accomplished by physical descriptions, that is, by listing all behaviors at the microlevel that children exhibit in a particular context. The microlevel categories are then aggregated, empirically, into mutually exclusive macrolevel categories. The categories used in this chapter are derived from the playground observations of Humphreys and Smith (1987) and Pellegrini (1988). These behaviors are listed in Table 4.1.

TABLE 4.1

Inventory of Children's Playground Behaviors

Passive-Noninteractive	Fixate	Balance
Sit	Take	Jump
Stand	Grab	Slide
Lie	Push	Swing
Eat	Swear at	Climb
Watch person	Insult	Roll/spin
Look at place		Piggy-back
Sedentary	*Distress*	Dance
Wait turn	Cry/sob	
		Games-with-rules
Passive-Interactive	*R&T*	Jump rope
Talk with adult	Tease	Compete
Talk with peer	Hit/kick	Tag
Contact/comfort	Poke	Clap/sing
Hug	Pounce	Ballgame
Groom	Chase	Catch
Walk/look	Hold/grab	Follow leader
Dress	Pull/push	
	Carry	*Object Play*
Observer/directed	Sneak up	Throw object
Attend to observer	Play fight	Active
		Quiet
Adult-organized	*Vigorous play*	Small motor
Official game	Walk	Large motor
	Run	Active
Aggressive	Skip/hop	Quiet
Hit with closed hand	Walk/follow	
Frown		

Further, the consequence of specific behaviors are considered. By using consequential and physical description I aimed to make the category system exhaustive.

The research reported in this chapter also extended the playground literature by describing the extent to which boys and girls at different grade levels acted on the playground at recess. As I noted in earlier chapters, these are two very important variables in relation to playground behavior. Briefly, boys, much more than girls, prefer to be outdoors, and when they are outdoors they are also more physically active than girls. Consequently, we would expect boys and girls to self-select themselves into very different parts of the playground and to exhibit correspondingly different types of behavior. Boys, for example, might be expected to sample more parts of the playground than girls do; relatedly, boys may exhibit more vigorous behavior because they choose to play in parts of the playground that support that type of behavior, such as the swings or the slides. Regarding variations in behavior due to age, or grade level. we might expect older children to engage in more cooperative games than do younger children.

In this chapter I will explore relations between behaviors exhibited on the playground and children's social competence in school settings. By "social competence" I mean the ways in which children adapt to school. Adaptation to school involves the ability to get along with peers and teachers, as well as more traditional dimensions of achievement-related behavior. Recess behavior, I think, should be a particularly good indicator of children's social competence to the extent that it is a highly motivating situation marked by minimal adult involvement; during recess children must interact with each other on their own terms. Thus, children should exhibit high levels of social competence at recess because they are motivated to interact (to the extent that it is an enjoyable context) with peers with minimal adult intervention. The tack I take in this chapter involves relating aspects of children's behavior to contemporaneous and longitudinal measures of social competence.

The measures of social competence I used include popularity with peers, ability to solve hypothetical social problems, teacher rating of the child's personality, and the child's academic achievement. All of these measures were collected across a two-year period to produce a longitudinal picture of children's social competence across the elementary school years. The longitudinal nature of the data allowed me to begin to make inferences about developmental processes per se and the causal relations between behavior and social competence.

Method

Subjects

There were 94 children whose parents consented to their participation in this research. The research site was a public elementary school, grades K-5, in Athens, GA. Children were recruited from two classrooms at each of three grade levels: K, 2, and 4. There were 35 from K (18 boys), 30 from grade 2 (16 boys), and 29 from grade 4 (14 boys, 15 girls).

Procedures

Children were observed during their daily recess period from October through May across a two-year period. Recess lasted for 25 minutes and was situated immediately following the lunch period for each grade. There were about 120-150 children on the playground at any one time and they were supervised by three to five female teacher's aides.

The children had free access to all aspects of the playground, which included the following components: a blacktop area of about 1,000 square yards, a contemporary playscape situated in a pine forest, about 350 square yards, and a grassy area, of about 200 square yards, separating the playscape from the blacktop. Children's behavior was recorded by four observers using scan sampling and instantaneous recording techniques. Observers recorded the following information by whispering into a small tape recorder: the name and behavior of the focal child (from the listed behaviors in Table 4.1), playground location, number of boys and girls in the immediate vicinity of the focal child, and the reactors' behaviors. Each child was observed at least 100 times across the school year.

Measures

Popularity. Children's popularity was assessed using socio-metric nomination procedures pioneered by Coie and Dodge (1983). Individual children were seated at a table before a display of individual pictures of all their classmates. They were first asked to point to and name each child, and then they were asked to nominate three children they liked best and three they liked least. This procedure, in addition to yielding "likes least" and "likes most" scores, also yields social preference scores (likes most – likes least) and social impact scores (likes most + likes least).

Hypothetical social problem solving. Spivak and Shure's (1979) procedure for assessing children's ability to generate a variety of solutions for hypothetical social problems was used. In this procedure an experimenter presented individual children with five separate pictures of a child trying to get a toy from a peer and five separate pictures of a children trying to avoid being reprimanded by his or her mother. Children were asked to generate as many different solutions to the problems as possible. Children's responses were tape-recorded and a variety of different responses was scored.

Children's Behavior Questionnaire. The Children's Behavior Questionnaire was developed by Rutter (1967) as part of his studies of children's adjustment in schools. This teacher-completed questionnaire has 26 items scored on a Likert-type scale from 0 (does not apply) to 2 (certainly applies) and yields to factors: an antisocial factor and a neurotic factor.

Achievement. During years 1 and 2 children's achievement was assessed with the California Achievement Test; the aggregate (standardized) score of all mathematics and reading/language subtests was used in analyses.

Results/Discussion of Contemporaneous Data

Initially the effects of grade level (3:K, 2, and 4), gender (2), and playground location (3: playscape, grassy area, blacktop) on children's behavior was assessed. Because of the large number of behavioral variables and the corresponding threat of Type I error, a multivariate analysis of variance (MANOVA) was calculated initially and significant effects for location $F (38,210) = 4.67, p < .0001$, and gender, $F (19,69) = 1.70, p < .05$, were detected; no significant effect for grade was detected nor were interactive effects significant. Subsequently, univariate location × gender ANOVAs were calculated on each of the behavioral categories; these results are displayed in Table 4.2.

TABLE 4.2

Location and Gender Effects on Playground Behavior

Behavior	Location		Gender	
	F	Contrast	F	Contrast
Passive-noninteractive	33.27**	PS > SF	0.22	ns
Passive-interactive	9.85**	PS + SF >	0.77	ns
Observer-directed	1.30	BT	83	ns
Adult-organized	0.72	ns	0.42	ns
Aggressive	2.61	ns	0.10	ns
R&T	9.81**	ns	3.55*	B > G
Vigorous play	34.60**	PS = SF >	3.27*	B > G
Games with rules	1.50	BT	0.16	ns
Object play	0.00	PS > SF +	0.00	ns
Role play	0.14	BT	1.19	ns
Variety	56.14**	ns	0.00	ns
		ns		
		ns		
		PS > SF >		
		BT		

Notes: $df = 1,87$ for location and for gender.
*PS = playscape; SF = soft, grassy area; BT = blacktop. B = boy, G = girl.
*$p < .05$ **$p < .01$

Different Behavior in Different Parts of the Playground

These findings, not surprisingly, indicated that children's behavior on the playground varies as a function of gender and playground location. Obviously, the gender and location effects are interrelated to the extent that boys and girls, having free choice to go where they wanted to go on the playground, self-selected themselves into different playground locations. This gender-related self-selection *and* the locations elicited the behaviors observed. The intercorrelations between gender and location are most clear in the case of vigorous play and R&T. In both cases effects for gender and location were observed. Boys typically self-selected themselves onto the playscape and engaged in vigorous and rough behavior.

The ways in which children used the same environment in different ways is illustrated very nicely by the playscape data. The playscape was the most popular area. It also was the site of both physically vigorous forms of behavior and very passive forms of behavior; indeed, it was the site of the most varied types of behavior. This finding is an important illustration of a way in which individuals define the environments in which they interact. That is, individuals' behavior, on playgrounds at least, is not *coerced* by the environment, as some environmental psychologists state (e.g., Gump, 1988). Children seem to define their environments in ways that suit them best. Environments are probably more coercive where they have explicit standing rules of behavior, such as in the cafeteria.

Relatedly, these results illustrate the artificiality of dichotomizing physical and social dimensions of the environment. First, it was clear from our data that different children chose different environments; thus, different environments are relevant to different children. Specific types of children choose to go into specific environments and, further, once there they shaped those niches to their liking, by either choosing to take certain children with them or by interacting in specified ways while there (Scarr & McCartney, 1983). Second, it was also clear that even when different children are in the same environment, they may and do define it very differently. Different children see different aspects of the same environment as differently relevant, and consequently "affording" different opportunities to different children (Greeno, 1991). In short, dichotomizing children from their physical environments is artificial; they are interactive. This should be kept in mind as we talk about the ways in which children act on different parts of the playground.

Variation in Behavior by Grade and Gender

The absence of a grade effect on playground behavior was a surprise. I would have expected, following Piaget (1965), children, as they grow older, to engage in more cooperative interaction and rule-governed games. Correspondingly, I would have expected R&T to decline with age. The reason for the lack of age effects on children's games may have been due to the absence of game-related props, such as basketball courts and hopscotch areas, on the playground. Regarding R&T, it may be that it declines, as I will note in Chapters 9 and 10, with the onset of adolescence. During adolescence boys move from male-segregated groups where they engage in vigorous activities, like R&T, to gender-integrated groups where less physically active forms of social interaction take place. In short, the absence of a grade effect on R&T may have been due to a relatively restricted grade range.

Equally probable may be the explanation that a school policy restricting aggression also restricted R&T. In this school, as in many other schools across our nation, aggression has been an increasing problem. The nightly news is too often replete with cases of gang violence in schools and shootouts in schoolyards. In their concern with such increasing levels of aggression, schools may be paying increased attention to less severe, but still very serious, forms of aggression, such as bullying, which often occurs on the playground (Smith & Thompson, 1990). In an effort to check increasing levels of aggression, teachers and other playground supervisors may also be checking play fighting. This seems reasonable in light of recent findings suggesting that teachers do not accurately discriminate play fighting from real fighting (Smees, 1992).

Contemporaneous Relations between
Playground Behavior and Social Competence.

Next, the relations between playground behaviors and dimensions of children's social competence will be examined. Girls' playground behavior did not correlate significantly with the measures of social competence employed in this study. The paucity of correlation for girls, compared to boys, may be the result of my choice of methods or due to the fact that the playground is a male-preferred, not a female-preferred, area. In other words, because girls do not enjoy the playground and its corresponding activities as much as boys do, this may mean that is is not a place where girls choose to exhibit their social skills. Girls may choose to exhibit their skills in areas, such as indoor, social interaction, that are more motivating to them. Indeed, other research (e.g., Lockheed, Harris, & Nemiceff, 1983; Pellegrini & Perlmutter, 1989) suggests that girls actually suppress their exhibition of competence in male-preferred situations. This, it should be noted, is another example of the interactive relations between environmental and personal variables.

Boys' playground behaviors, on the other hand, related to a number of aspects of social competence. Specifically, boys' vigorous and R&T behavior was positively and significantly correlated with "likes least" nominations ($r = .38, p < .01$) and variety of social problem solutions ($r = .30, p < .05$), respectively, and negatively and significantly correlated with social impact ($r = -.29, p <. 05$); boys' aggression was negatively and significantly related to "likes most" nominations ($r = -.30, p < .05$). Generally, then, boys' vigorous behavior correlated with not being popular. Boys who engage in this form of behavior may not have the social cognitive skills to engage in more-rule-governed behaviors, like games. Vigorous behavior was, in turn, not significantly correlated with games.

There are at least two explanations for these negative relations between aggressive/vigorous behaviors and social competence. The first involves a social information processing deficit model whereby deficits in processing social information were reflected in the aggressive and vigorous behavior and inability to interact successfully with peers.

At another level it may be the case that these aggressive children did not suffer from a deficit in processing social information but instead consciously used aggression as a way by which to acquire resources, such as attention and access to games. As I will show in Chapter 11, this seems to be the case during early adolescence. That is aggressive boys do not seem deficient in processing social information to the extent that they reliably choose a weaker child to bully.

The relation between R&T and social problem solving during the primary and middle school years will be discussed in greater detail in Chapters 8 and 11, respectively. Suffice it to say for the time being that the flexible dimension of R&T and the different roles enacted may be responsible for R&T relating to flexible social problem-solving ability.

Boys' R&T was also correlated ($r = -.26, p < .06$) with a standardized aggregate measure of achievement. The negative correlation, though only approaching significance, may indicate that both adjusted boys (such as sociometrically popular boys) and maladjusted boys (such as sociometrically rejected boys) engage in R&T at near equal rates. While this research will be discussed in detail in Chapter 8, it follows that rejected and popular boys, respectively, do poorly and well in school.

Interestingly, girls' games were correlated (*also* r = .26, p < .06) with achievement. This relation is certainly consistent with the Piagetian (1965) position that game playing has a cognitive component and play ground games like hopscotch (with grids made by the children themselves) and jump rope reflect and/or exercise cognitive processes.

Results/Discussion: Longitudinal Data

Next I will discuss the longitudinal relations between playground behavior in year 1 and social competence in year 2. First, I will present the year-to-year stability of the behavioral and social competence measures. Then, I will present predictive relations between behaviors and social competence. Because main effects due to gender were observed, data were analyzed separately for boys and girls.

Year-to-Year Stability

For both boys and girls there was very little year-to-year inter-correlation of behavior. Even for aggression, which has been shown to be stable across childhood (Olweus, 1979), the correlation was nonsignificant. Changes in school policy within each year, for example, shifts in the personnel supervising the recess periods and the opening of a new playing field, may have been responsible for the lack of year-to-year stability. A more likely explanation, however, at least in the case of aggression was the low rates and lack of variation in aggression, possibly because aggression was discouraged by school policy.

Next, the stability of the measures of social competence. For boys, social problem solving was very stable across a one-year lag (r = .68, p < .0001), as were the following: "likes least" nominations (r = .49, p < .005), social preference (r = .50, p < .0004), and antisocial ratings by teachers (r = .41, p < .02). In short, negative aspects of boys' social competence were stable. This is consistent with the extant literature (Asher & Coie, 1990) and helps clarify my finding that aggressive behavior was not stable. It was probably the case that children were not aggressive on the playground because of school policy and supervision. Across the school day and in various, less-well-supervised situations, such as the restrooms, buses, and walk-ing home boys probably had a chance to exhibit more antisocial behavior. These less obvious, and more difficult to record through playground observations, forms of behavior were probably reflected in the peer nominations.

For girls, social problem solving was not correlated from year 1 to year 2 as it was for boys. The only aspects of girls' social compe-tence correlated from year 1 to year 2 were social preference (r = .33, p < .04) and the antisocial personality factor on the Rutter ques-tionnaire (r = .81, p < .0001). As was the case with boys, dimensions of antisocial behavior seem to be very stable as was social preference.

Regarding the stability of antisocial factors, it is probably the case that this stability is due to both biological and environmental factors, that is, aggression has a biological component to the extent that certain hormonal events are correlated with aggressive behav-ior (Olweus, 1988) but hormones can *both* react to and determine aggression. Relatedly, a stable environment, such as parental social-ization strategies can be responsible for stability in aggression. The finding that aggression is stable from an early age underscores the importance of trying to help children who show aggressive tendencies as early as possible. Effective and reliable ways of identifying such children include sociometric nominations and peer questionnaires. While peer rejection is a reliable predictor of aggression and later social maladjustment (Parker & Asher, 1987), other factors, like level of social withdrawal, also relate to rejection. Asking children who they like and dislike should, then, be complemented by asking them who hits, who doesn't hit, and who keeps to themselves.

A word of caution, however, must be voiced in this area of iden-tification, treatment, and remediation. It is very important, from a civil liberties perspective, that "at-risk" classification for certain problems, such as aggression, not be merely a result of children's membership in specific cultural groups. That is, just because a cor-relation exists between aggression and membership in a certain group, such as Native Americans or African Americans, should not result in classifying all children in that group as at-risk for this and related problems.

Another warning involves making causality assumptions. The analyses presented here are only correlational: though they have antecedent-consequence relations, we should not assume that the antecedent *causes* the consequence. It may be the case that unmea-sured factors or year-to-year stability of the criterion measure are responsible for these correlations. For example, if we have a significant positive correlation from year 1 game behavior to year 2 social preference, an unmeasured factor (such as social perspective-taking skills) may be responsible for the relation, such that game-playing ability is just an artifact of what sociocentric children do. Similarly, in the case of year-to-year stability, the above-noted hypothetical relation could be due to the fact that social preference is stable from year to year and that popular children tend to play games, not that game playing results in popularity.

Predictive Relations

I now move to a discussion of the correlations between year 1 behavior and year 2 social competence. As in the earlier cases, separate analyses for boys and girls will be presented. I will begin with the boys. The relative frequency with which boys in year 1 engaged in cooperative games predicted *negatively* ($r = -.33$, $p < .06$) their number of "likes least" nominations, their being rated by their teachers as antisocial ($r = -.38$, $p < .03$), and their year 2 standardized achievement ($r = -.37$, $p < .03$). Thus, while game playing at recess predicted that children would not be aggressive or disliked, it also predicted that boys would achieve at low levels.

The games variable is obviously a gross variable to the extent that lots of very different games are included. In order to uncover clearer implications here we need to know more about the games the children played. For example, some games, like tag, are of low cognitive level, while others, like hide'n'seek, are more strategic. Children engaging in the low-level games would be expected to be low achievers, while children engaged in the more strategic games would be expected to be high achievers. Research of the ethnographic type that describes the kinds of games that children play is needed; as a complement to this research we also need to know the trajectory of the children playing different sorts of games.

The relations between games and social competence seems a bit more clear to the extent that nonaggressive children play more games. That playground games are typically social indicates that in order to partake in these activities children must be liked, or more accurately, not be disliked, and must be nonaggressive. Aggressive and disliked children tended to be avoided by their peers.

The results for girls is similar to those for boys to the extent that girls' games predicted "likes most" nominations ($r = .28$, $p < .09$) and social impact ($r = .36$, $p < .02$), and their R&T predicted social problem solving ($r = .29$, $p < .08$) and neurotic personality ($r = .34$, $p < .04$). Thus, girls engaging in socially cooperative interaction were good social problem solvers and were liked by their peers. Their teachers, however, thought they were neurotic. While these girls may indeed have been neurotic, it may have been the case that the teachers, most of whom were female, rated girls who engaged in a typically male activity, R&T, as neurotic.

In the cases of both boys and girls, we need in-depth descriptions of the kinds of games they play and how these games, in turn, reflect on and predict social cognition.

Conclusion

We have seen how children's behavior on the playground varies considerably by gender and playground location. These behaviors, in turn, have interesting corelations with aspects of children's social competence and achievement. That significant relations exist between aspects of playground behavior and traditional achievement measures is very interesting. Does it mean that children are actually learning something out there? Or, more conservatively, does it mean that they are practicing something important they have learned elsewhere? In either case, these results suggest that recess behavior has important implications for traditional measures of achievement. It is perhaps less surprising that children's playground behavior related to aspects of social competence, such as popularity, social problem solving, and personality factors. After all, recess is, or should be, a time for children to interact among themselves. It is relatively easy, though very labor intensive, to identify children who interact well, as well as those who do not. If educators think it is important to educate the "whole child," then these social concerns should also be educational concerns. Following this view, educators would think it important to promote the cognitive as well as the social skills.

I also noted that the playground was a motivating context. Children generally enjoy their time on the playground and exhibit relatively high levels of competence so that they can participate fully. This sort of information can be useful in other areas of education and child development, particularly in areas relating to assessment of children. Currently, assessment of children in educational settings is being reconsidered. Part of the debate involves the role of paper-and-pencil tests with young children. Young children, as we all know, are unreliable test takers, possibly because they are minimally motivated to perform in these settings. These problems can be minimized, possibly, if we chose real and analogue situations, like games on playgrounds, which children find motivating.

References

Asher, S., & Coie, J. (1990). (Eds.). *Peer rejection in childhood*. New York: Cambridge University Press.

Greeno, J. (1990). Number sense as situated knowing in a conceptual domain. *Journal of Research in Mathematic Education.*, 22, 170-218.

Gump, P. (1988). Ecological psychology and issues of play. In M. Bloch & A. D. Pellegrini (eds.), *The ecological context of children's play* (pp. 35-36). Norwood, NJ: Ablex.

Lockheed, M., Harris, A., & Nemiceff, W. (1983). Sex and social influence: Does sex function as a status characteristic in mixed-sex groups of children? *Journal of Educational Psychology*, 75, 877-888.

Olweus, D. (1979). Stability and aggressive reaction patterns in males: A review. *Psychological Bulletin*, 86, 852-875.

Parker, J., & Asher, S. (1987). Peer reltions and later personal adjustment: Are low-accepted children at-risk? *Psychological Bulletin*, 102, 357-389.

Pellegrini, A. D., & Perlmutter, J. (1989). Classroom contextual effects on children's play. *Develpomental Psychology*, 25, 289-296.

Piaget, J. (1965). *The moral development of the child*. New York: Free Press.

Scarr, S., & McCartney, K. (1983). How people make their own environments. *Child Development*, 54, 424-435.

Smees, R. (1992). *An investigation into the effects of participation and non-participation on the perceptions of playfighting and real fighting*. Unpublished B.A. dissertation, Sheffield University (U.K.).

Smith, P. I., & Thompson, D. (1990). *Practical approaches to bullying*. London: David Fulton.

5

The Effects of Recess Timing on Elementary School Children's Recess and Classroom Behavior

Introduction

As I noted in preceding chapters, a number of within-school factors affect children's behavior on the playground at recess time. In this chapter the effect of one important, but not frequently studied, within-school variable will be examined: recess timing. By "recess timing" I mean the point in the school day when recess is held and the duration of the recess period itself. This issue of recess timing is extremely important from both an educational policy perspective and from a child development perspective.

Educational policy should be concerned with recess timing. As I noted in Chapter 1, anecdotal evidence reported by Blatchford (1988) in the United Kingdom, suggests that teachers and children are concerned with this issue to the extent that some say recess disrupts the flow of work while others say it provides a needed break from sedentary classroom work. Thus there seems to be disagreement about the role of a very important (important in terms of its ubiquity) aspect of the school day. Answers to this sort of question, it seems to me, can and should be addressed empirically. These questions, in turn, should be guided by child development theory.

The importance of the recess period in primary school curricula is typically justified with a variant of Surplus Energy Theory, popular in the nineteenth century (Spencer, 1898). This theory posits a positive relation between immediately preceding confinement and subsequent activity because of the individual's need to release surplus energy that accumulates during confinement. Contemporary folk variants of this theory often speak of a need to "let off steam." Despite its intuitive appeal, the Surplus Energy Theory does not have scientific credibility. For example, the theory does not explain

y tired animals still play in the face of an "interesting" stimuli
Burghardt, 1984). Further, the building up and discharging of
energy is physiologically unsound and there are no criteria for what
constitutes a surplus of energy (Smith & Hagan, 1980). This is not to
say that energy-related issues are not relevant to the study of play.
For example, children's nutritional status affects their level of stored
energy, which in turn relates to their degree of vigorous behavior;
thus, malnourished children should exhibit low levels of vigor
(Burghardt, 1984).

Another psychological justification for the importance of
recess can be derived from Novelty Theory (Berlyne, 1960, 1966;
Ellis, 1984; Fein, 1981). Novelty Theory argues that children's
behavior during an activity is initially determined by the degree of
novelty inherent in that activity. As novelty diminishes, children
habituate to or become bored with a particular activity, and their
concentration on that activity wanes; unless prevented, they will
eventually seek novelty by switching to another activity. Children
often seek novelty through some form of motor and/or social play in
order to keep their central nervous systems at optimal levels of
arousal (Baldwin & Baldwin, 1978). If we apply Novelty Theory to
children in classrooms and at recess, we would expect them to
habituate to their immediate school environments as a function of
time and then seek novelty in another activity. Further, Novelty
Theory suggests that children deprived of a stimulating environment for a longer period of time preceding recess, when compared
to other children deprived for a shorter period, should seek novelty
at a greater rate.

Recess typically provides novelty because its demand charac-
teristics are very different from those of the classroom; for example,
recess activities are generally self-defined, physically active, and
involve spontaneous peer interaction, while classroom activities are
more sedentary and teacher-directed. In short, Novelty Theory predicts that children should become less attentive to seat work as a
function of time; that is, the longer they sit in the classroom, the
less attentive and more restless they should become.
Correspondingly, children should seek more novelty on the playground, as a function of preceding confinement; that is, longer, compared to shorter, periods wherein children are confined to sedentary seat work should result in more novelty seeking on the
playground. Further, they should habituate to the playground at
recess as a function of time; in other words, with time the playground too becomes less novel.

Obviously, the effects of recess can be determined in a number of ways. One option might involve studying a recess group and another no-recess group. In this way the extreme effects of recess deprivation could be charted. Another, and more ecologically valid, option involves varying the timing of recess such that different groups of children are deprived of recess for a fixed period. The ecological validity of this approach, compared to the first approach, is evidenced by the presence of recess in one form or another in almost all American elementary schools (National Association of Elementary School Principals Principals' Practice Survey, 1990; also see Chapter 1). Further, some schools often vary the actual times that classes go outdoors for recess depending on specific scheduling constraints; thus varying the time that children go out to recess should be part of the normal school day for most children.

Elementary school children's reactions to differing periods of confinement before recess varies systematically as a function of gender. First, it is well documented that elementary school boys, compared to girls, are more physically active (Eaton & Enns, 1986; Maccoby & Jacklin, 1974). This difference has been implicated in gender differences in classroom behavior (Brophy & Putnam, 1979); for example, these differences may cause boys to be less attentive during seat work and more restless than girls. Consequently, we would expect gender differences regarding children's task-relevant classroom behavior preceding recess. Further, that elementary school boys are more physically active than girls (Eaton & Enns, 1986) suggests that boys, more than girls, may seek novelty on the playground through physically vigorous activities. That girls engage in more sedentary and social sedentary activities than boys suggests that they may seek novelty through those means.

To my knowledge, only one other study has empirically examined the effects of preceding classroom confinement, or exercise deprivation, on children's outdoor play. Smith and Hagan (1980), in a well-conducted six-week field experiment, examined the effects of longer (90 minutes) and shorter (45 minutes) confinement periods on British preschool children's exercise play (e.g., running, jumping, wrestling, climbing) on the playground. Confinement was defined as indoor classroom work. Results revealed that more and higher levels of exercise play were exhibited by the longer confinement group, compared to the shorter confinement group. Also, exercise play decreased during recess as a function of time spent on the playground. No gender differences were observed for these preschool children.

While important, the results of the Smith and Hagan (1980) study have limited application to the case of American elementary schools. First, preschool children are different (e.g., in terms of activity level and social interaction skills) than elementary school children. Therefore, more research with this group is needed. Related to this age issue is the fact that minimal gender differences are observed for physical activity during the preschool period, but such gender differences become apparent in the elementary school period (Eaton & Enns, 1986; Smith & Connolly, 1980; Smith & Hagan, 1980). Further, Smith and Hagan only reported exercise data. It may be true, as suggested above, that boys and girls "rebound" from confinement and seek novelty in different ways. Girls may seek novelty through more sedentary means than boys do. Consequently, both active and sedentary behaviors should be important topics of study.

Lastly, and very important from an educational perspective, Smith and Hagan's data do not inform us as to the relations between *recess* behavior and *classroom* behavior. Again, novelty theory provides guidance for important questions in these areas. For example, are children less attentive to seat work the longer they are confined? And what is the relation between what goes on at recess and classroom behavior following recess?

The second objective of this study was directly related to the point of relating recess behavior to classroom behavior. Recent work with a sample of elementary school children showed that children's playground behavior was a reliable predictor of their academic status (see Chapter 6). This work suggests that children who engage in reciprocal social interaction with peers, when compared to those who engaged in nonsocial behavior, are judged to be more socially competent by both their teachers and their peers and also have higher achievement levels. I will argue in the next chapter, from a social competence perspective, that the skills necessary to sustain cooperative peer interaction on the playground, for example, reciprocal role-taking, perspective-taking, and conversational skills, are also necessary for traditional academic tasks. Consequently, I predict that social behavior on the playground should predict post-recess task-relevant behavior. While the present study does not address the interrelations between playground and classroom social cognitive processes, it does allow us to begin to understand the ways by which recess timing affects children's behaviors in each context.

In summary, I will first address the decrement of task-relevant classroom behavior as a function of gender and confinement time before recess. Boys should be less attentive than girls, and all children should be less attentive as the duration of confinement increases. Further, I expected children's recess behavior to be affected by confinement: the longer period should elicit more novelty seeking in the form of both physically active and sedentary behaviors. Boys should seek novelty through physical activity, while girls should seek novelty through more sedentary means. Lastly, social behavior at recess should predict postrecess task-relevant behavior.

Method

Subjects

Subjects represented the population of a third grade public school classroom in a small city in the southeastern United States. There were a total of 23 children (14 males and 9 females) in this sample, with a mean age of 9.4 years. The composition of the classroom was heterogeneous in terms of ability (*Mean* I.Q. = 96.62, *SD* = 16.9). In this within-subjects design, each child was exposed to both the longer and shorter confinement treatment conditions. The children were observed for a total of 14 weeks, from late winter to late spring. The schedule for this particular classroom was as follows:

7:55—Class begins
8:00-8:30—Spelling
8:30-10:30/11:00—Reading/language arts or mathematics (10:30 for short confinement/11:00 for long)
10:30/11:00-11:00/11:30—Recess for short and long confinement, respectively
11:00 or 11:30-12:00—Mathematics or Reading/Language Arts (depending on preceding condition)

The instructional regimen for the 30 minutes directly preceding and succeeding the recess period was standardized for all children; that is, all children were given the same seat work to complete. The subject matter taught before and after recess was counterbalanced. During the times that children were in their classrooms they were expected to sit quietly at their desks and to work on written assignments such as language arts or math.

At recess children were free to engage in physical and social activities or to just be alone; only antisocial behavior was discouraged by school policy. Children were supervised by their classroom teacher on the playground. Further, there often was one or two other classrooms on the playground at the same time. The playground was large and had two distinct components: a 2½ acre field that included a contemporary playscape and a blacktop area (13 × 28 meters) that included a basketball court and a four-square area. This large space minimized crowding effects that may have arisen.

Procedure

As part of the regular school testing program the Iowa Test of Basic Skills (ITBS, 1986) was administered in April of the study year; the verbal and nonverbal Cognitive Ability Test standard scores were provided by this test. For the purposes of this study the mean of these two standardized scores was used to statistically equate children's ability for certain analyses.

Treatment Conditions

There were two treatment conditions: a shorter confinement period and a longer confinement period. As noted above, the shorter period involved children engaged in seat work from 8-10:30 A.M., or 2½ hours, and the longer period had children engaged in seat work from 8-11:00 A.M., or 3 hours. Each child was exposed to both treatments. The order in which the treatments were administered was counterbalanced across the 14-week observation period. Observations were conducted by three observers. A 4-week familiarization period preceded the actual data collection so as to minimize observer obtrusiveness and sharpen observation skills.

Observational Procedures

All children were observed in three separate situations: for 23 minutes in the classroom, during the time directly preceding recess; during the first 23 minutes of a 25-30 minute recess period; and for 23 minutes directly following recess in the classroom. Further, data were collected only on days when there was outdoor recess. As I noted above, children in the classroom were given standardized seat work.

For each of the three situations, children were observed 23 times using scan sampling and instantaneous recording rules (Martin & Bateson, 1986). More specifically, a total of 23 separate lists of names drawn from the class list were constructed (counterbalancing lists within and across situations) for each of the three situations: prerecess, postrecess, and recess itself. Each child was sampled one time in each of these situations per day, for a total of 23 samples per child per situation. This procedure eliminated problems of interdependent within-day observations of individual subjects because they were only observed one time in each situation, that is, prerecess, postrecess, and at recess. A different child was sampled every 60 seconds. Children's behaviors (listed below) was recorded instantaneously at those 60-second points, for 23 data collection points within each situation/day. Further, each child was observed in the 1st through 23rd observational positions for each situation; that is, each child was observed at each interval in each situation. This enabled us to track behaviors across 23 1-minute intervals in each situation and eliminate a time interval × individual confound.

Children's behaviors in the classroom and on the playground were recorded on checklists. A series of checklists for the subjects to be observed on specific days were prepared in advance. The checklist used for both pre- and postrecess behavior included the following behaviors:

Fidget: This behavior was defined as moves in seat; taps feet, hands, desk, pencil, and the like; scratches head or other body parts. Fidget was scored from 1 to 7, with 1 as no fidgeting and 7 when all of the listed behaviors were observed.

Concentration: This classroom behavior was defined as degree of attention to the seat work, or directness of gaze to work. Scored from 1 (low concentration) to 7 (high concentration). A score of 7 indicated that a child was directly facing the task. A score of 1 indicated a subject's head was turned at any point among the 90 degrees perpendicular to the task; behind the higher scores represented varying, incremental degrees of head-to-task gaze.

Duration interval: This was the order in the observational sequence of the 23 minutes directly preceding recess. This varied from 1 to 23 minutes in duration.

The recess behaviors were also coded on separate checklists and included six behaviors:

Nonsocial exercise: This was defined, following Smith and Hagan (1980), as gross body and/or muscular activity, for example, running, jumping, throwing, climbing, or wrestling. Exercise was scored as nonsocial if a child was exhibiting the above-

noted behaviors alone or in the absence of direct and reciprocal eye or linguistic contact with other children. Nonsocial
exercise for each child was scored as yes or no, yielding a
score from 0 to 23. This score was then transformed into a
relative frequency score, that is, each boy's score was related
to all boys' scores, because of the unequal number of boys and
girls.

Social exercise: This was coded as social if children were exchanging
language, gestures, or gazes. Where no such exchanges were
noted,the behavior was coded nonsocial. Like nonsocial exercise, relative frequencies were the units of analysis.

Vigor of exercise: This was defined, following Maccoby and Jacklin
(1987), as activity intensity. This score ranged from 1 (low) to 7
(high).

Nonsocial sedentary: This was defined as nonstrenuous activity,
such as walking, sitting, standing, and so on. Nonsocial sedentary, like nonsocial exercise, was scored as nonsocial if children were alone or they did not make reciprocal contact with
others. Relative frequencies were the units of analysis.

Social sedentary: This was defined according to the same sedentary
conditions as nonsocial sedentary but in these cases children
were interacting with others, using gestures, language, or
exchanging gazes.

Duration interval within recess: This was defined as it was for classroom behaviors, varying from 1 to 23.

Observers were trained before the actual data collection began
in individual training sessions involving the discussion of inclusive
and exclusive examples of each category. During the initial 4-week
familiarization period, observers coded observational data (not
included in analyses) and discussed areas of agreement and disagreement. Three observers collected data simultaneously across a 4-
week period. One observer was not aware of the hypotheses of the
study, thus, I was able to check for observer bias. To conduct this
check, I compared the two sets of observations separately for prerecess and postrecess and recess behaviors. No differences were
detected. At midpoint in the study, after a reliability check session,
similar discussions occurred. Reliability checks were conducted
among three observers. Reliability coefficients (*kappa*) were calculated from a sample of observation 161 recess focal samples and 322
pre- and postrecess focal samples. The reliability coefficients for each
category follow:

Fidget: .83
Concentration: .77
Duration Interval: 1.0
Exercise/Nonsocial: .94
Exercise/Social: .86
Vigor: .73
Sedentary/Nonsocial: .92
Sedentary/Social: .91

Results

First I examined the main and interactive effects of gender (2), condition (2: longer, shorter), and prerecess time duration (23 one-minute intervals) on two separate measures of children's prerecess behavior: concentration and fidgeting. Further, children's Cognitive Ability Test scores were statistically controlled because they were significantly related to fidgeting ($r = -.22$) and concentration ($r = .25$). Gender was a between-subjects variable; condition and time duration were both within-subjects variables; and Cognitive Ability Test score was used as a covariate. For fidgeting, significant main effects were observed, for gender, $F(1,355) = 3.86, p < .05$, and condition, $F(1,355) = 4.91, p < .02$, using repeated measures analysis of covariance (ANCOVA); cognitive ability also made a significant contribution, $F(1,355) = 9.97, p < .001$. The R2 for the whole model was .29. Post hoc analyses were conducted following the Student-Newman-Keuls procedure, with an .05 *alpha*. Boys ($M = 3.33$) fidgeted significantly more than girls ($M = 2.75$); all children fidgeted significantly more in the long confinement condition ($M = 3.32$) than in the short condition ($M = 2.83$).

The ANCOVA for prerecess concentration revealed a condition × duration effect that was only approaching significance, $F(1,355) = 1.45, p < .09$; the R2 for the whole model was .30. The interactive effect suggests that children in the longer confinement group ($M = 2.94$ across the first 8-minute segment), compared to those in the shorter condition ($M = 3.54$ across the first 8-minute segment), concentrate less at the beginning of the duration and maintain that level throughout the whole 23 minutes ($M = 2.88$ and 2.80 for the second and third segments, respectively). The concentration levels of the children in the shorter confinement group dropped across all three segments ($M = 3.54, 2.85,$ and 2.77 for the three segments). The means for concentration are displayed in Table 5.1.

Next, I examined the effects of gender (2), condition (2), and recess duration (23 one-minute intervals) on the following aspects of recess behavior: nonsocial exercise play, social exercise play, vigor of exercise, nonsocial sedentary behavior, and social sedentary behavior. As in the above analyses, gender was a between-subjects variable and condition and duration were within-subjects variables in a series of repeated measures ANOVAs. Student-Newman-Keuls procedure, at .05, was used for post hoc analyses. Regarding nonsocial exercise, main effects of gender, $F(1,355) = 987.2$, $p < .0001$, and duration, $F(22,355) = 3.77$, $p < .0001$, and condition × duration effects, $F(21,355) = 6.30$, $p < .0001$, were observed; the R2 was .80. Boys ($M = .83$) engaged in significantly more nonsocial exercise play than did girls ($M = .46$).

Regarding the duration × condition interaction, between-condition comparisons at each interval revealed that there was more nonsocial exercise in the longer, compared to the shorter, condition, at the following intervals: 1, 11, 19, and 21. There was more exercise in the shorter, compared to the longer, condition in the following intervals: 6, 7, and 15. Within each condition, because of the large number of comparisons, I will present statistically significant differences between the following intervals: 1 and 8, 9 and 16, 17 and 23, and 1 and 23. In short, I compared the values at the beginning and end of the first, second, and final thirds of the duration intervals, and also compared the first and last intervals. Within the longer condition significant differences were observed between the beginning and end of the following intervals: 1 and 8, 17 and 23, and 1 and 23. No significant differences were observed within the shorter condition. When both conditions are combined, I found a difference between intervals 17 and 23. These data suggest, then, a general decrease in nonsocial exercise across duration and particularly in the longer condition. The means for nonsocial exercise are displayed in Table 5.2.

The variation in social exercise play as a function of gender, condition, and duration interval was also assessed, with a repeated measures ANOVA. Main effects were observed for gender, $F(1,355) = 673.83$, $p < .0001$, and interval duration, $F(22,355) = 2.89$, $p < .0001$; a significant condition × interval duration was also observed, $F(21,355) = 4.77$, $p < .0001$; the R2 was .74. Boys ($M = .82$) engaged in significantly more social exercise play than did girls ($M = .41$). In describing the interaction I followed the same procedure as above, by making comparisons between the beginning and final values of the following intervals: 1 and 8, 9 and 17, 17 and 23, and 1 and

TABLE 5.1

Means for Pre-Recess Concentration By Condition* and Duration Interval

	1	2	3	4	5	6	7	8	9	10	11	12	13	14	15	16	17	18	19	20	21	22	23	M
L	2.55	4.28	3.55	3.66	1.75	4.11	3.00	2.55	2.57	2.87	2.37	2.62	2.11	2.77	2.75	2.62	2.55	3.33	2.37	2.00	3.66	4.00	1.00	2.87
S	1.47	2.44	2.62	2.62	2.85	2.22	3.50	3.00	2.80	2.85	3.87	3.11	3.66	2.66	4.75	3.77	4.22	3.00	4.42	3.50	1.71	1.00	1.00	3.08
M	2.16	3.25	3.11	3.17	2.26	3.16	3.26	2.76	2.70	2.87	3.12	2.88	2.88	2.72	3.75	3.22	3.38	3.17	3.33	2.75	2.61	3.14	1.00	

*L = Long condition; S = Short condition; M = Mean across condition

TABLE 5.2

Means for Exercise Play By Condition* and Duration Interval

	1	2	3	4	5	6	7	8	9	10	11	12	13	14	15	16	17	18	19	20	21	22	23	M
L	.79	.68	.70	.76	.67	.60	.50	.64	.62	.64	.71	.71	.83	.55	.53	.59	.70	.76	.82	.65	.78	.51	.55	.67
S	.51	.75	.77	.62	.71	.82	.74	.62	.65	.56	.57	.65	.72	.77	.73	.58	.66	.68	.68	.72	.64	.52	.53	.67
M	.65	.71	.74	.68	.69	.72	.64	.63	.64	.60	.64	.68	.77	.66	.62	.58	.68	.72	.76	.69	.71	.51	.54	

*L = Long condition; S = Short condition; M = Mean across condition

23. The only significant difference was between intervals 1 and 23 within the longer condition. The means for social exercise are displayed in Table 5.3. Like nonsocial exercise, a general decline in social exercise was observed.

In the next series of analyses, the effects of gender, condition, and duration interval on vigor of exercise was examined. Significant effects for gender, F (1,355) = 104.59, p < .0001, and condition × duration, F (21,355) = 1.96, p < .008, were observed, with an R2 of .41 for the model. Boys (M = 3.75) were significantly more vigorous than girls (M = 1.50). Comparing conditions at each duration interval I found that the longer confinement condition, compared to the shorter condition, elicited significantly more vigorous exercise play at interval 1. At interval 22, the shorter condition elicited more vigorous exercise than the longer condition. There were no significant interval differences within the shorter condition. Within the longer condition, significant differences were observed between intervals 1 and 23 and 1 and 8. The means for vigor are presented in Table 5.4.

Nonsocial sedentary behavior was examined next with a gender × condition × duration interval repeated measures ANOVA. A significant main effect for gender, F (1,355) = 18.70, p < .0001, and a significant condition × duration interval interactive effect, F (21,355) = 1.61, p < .04, were observed; the R2 for the model was .28. Boys (M = .07) engaged in significantly more nonsocial sedentary behavior than did girls (M = .03). The longer, compared to the shorter, condition elicited more nonsocial sedentary behavior at interval 2 and 20 . The shorter condition, more than the longer condition, elicited more nonsocial sedentary behavior at interval 4. The means for nonsocial sedentary are displayed in Table 5.5.

Social sedentary behavior was analyzed next, again with a gender × condition × duration interval repeated measures ANOVA. Significant main effects were observed for gender, F (1,355) = 259.00, p < .0001, and duration interval, F (22,355) = 9.00, p < .0001, and a significant duration × condition interaction, F (21,355) = 13.32, p < .0001; the R2 for the model was .75. Girls (M = .50) engaged in significantly more social sedentary behavior than did boys (M = .09). The post hoc analyses on the duration interval main effect indicated a significant increase from intervals 1 to 23 and from 18 to 23. The duration × condition interaction analyses revealed significant between-condition differences at the following intervals: 1, 6, 7, 10, 13, 14, and 15. These means represent a general increase in social sedentary behavior across time. The means are displayed in Table 5.6.

recess, for example, outdoor vigorous play or opportunities to interact with peers, interact with other variables such as gender and temperament.

Next I examined the effects of gender, time at seat work preceding recess, and recess duration on children's recess behavior. These data, one could argue, provide insight into children's need for some other novel experience, such as recess. Biologists suggest, as I noted above, that the central nervous system is organized such that human beings, and other animals, try to maintain optimal levels of arousal through novelty seeking (Baldwin & Baldwin, 1972; Fagen, 1981). Consequently, need for novelty can be documented by the interrelation between confinement and seeking novelty and arousal. The data on the effects of confinement are consistent with novelty theory predictions to the extent that longer periods of confinement, compared to shorter periods, elicited more exercise, both social and nonsocial, and more vigorous exercise.

Further, a general decrement of exercise was observed across the recess period; this was particularly true in the longer confinement condition, compared to the shorter condition. Again, however, there were gender differences, with boys being more physically active than girls. Girls tended to be more sedentary than boys, but only on the social sedentary measure. That boys, more than girls, engaged in more nonsocial sedentary behavior may be an indicator of their having more difficulty in adjusting to the feminine bias of elementary schools (Minuchin & Shapiro, 1983). Specifically, boys often perceive school as a feminine, not a masculine, institution (Minuchin & Shapiro, 1983). Consistent with this hypothesis, nonsocial sedentary behavior has been found in previous research with elementary school children to be a reliable indicator of low social and academic status (see Chapter 6). This point will be further explicated below.

In short, timing of recess has a reliable effect on children's classroom and recess behavior, and the effects are mediated by children's gender. Future research in this area should address the optimal recess duration. That is, at what point during recess do children become bored? Is it after 15 minutes? 20 minutes? Relatedly, what other, different, experiences are novel for children? The gender differences reported above provide some guidance here to the extent that physical exercise is only one form of novelty seeking, the one used primarily by boys. Would opportunities to engage in student-directed peer discourse provide novel experiences for other children? If so, for what groups of children? Again, these are questions with important policy and curricular implications that can and should be

TABLE 5.3

Means for Relative Social Exercise Play By Condition* and Duration Interval

	1	2	3	4	5	6	7	8	9	10	11	12	13	14	15	16	17	18	19	20	21	22	23	M
L	.77	.65	.67	.73	.67	.57	.44	.63	.61	.59	.67	.68	.83	.50	.46	.57	.65	.74	.81	.62	.76	.47	.55	.64
S	.43	.75	.75	.58	.66	.82	.74	.59	.63	.55	.53	.61	.71	.75	.67	.52	.62	.65	.67	.70	.61	.52	.52	.63
M	.60	.70	.71	.64	.66	.70	.61	.61	.62	.57	.60	.64	.76	.63	.55	.55	.64	.70	.74	.67	.68	.48	.53	

*L = Long condition; S = Short condition; M = Mean across condition

TABLE 5.4

Means for Vigor of Exercise Play By Condition* and Duration Interval

	1	2	3	4	5	6	7	8	9	10	11	12	13	14	15	16	17	18	19	20	21	22	23	M
L	4.88	2.11	2.87	3.00	3.00	1.28	.42	1.55	2.22	2.11	3.66	3.14	1.87	2.62	2.66	2.00	3.33	3.33	3.23	2.42	4.50	1.40	1.40	2.64
S	1.55	4.37	4.00	3.55	3.00	3.25	3.33	2.10	2.55	2.77	1.88	2.88	2.88	3.62	3.57	2.37	2.28	3.14	2.75	2.62	2.83	5.00	5.00	2.93
M	3.22	3.17	3.47	3.29	3.00	2.33	2.11	1.82	2.38	2.44	2.77	3.00	2.41	3.12	3.06	2.17	2.87	3.25	3.00	2.53	3.66	2.00	2.00	2.00

*L = Long condition; S = Short condition; M = Mean across condition

TABLE 5.5

Means for Relative Sedentary Behavior by Condition* and Duration Interval

	1	2	3	4	5	6	7	8	9	10	11	12	13	14	15	16	17	18	19	20	21	22	23	M
L	.01	.05	.11	.02	.03	.06	.02	.03	.03	.11	.03	.02	.04	.11	.05	.04	.01	.05	.06	.12	.07	.04	.00	.05
S	.01	.03	.02	.14	.06	.02	.05	.08	.03	.04	.06	.05	.02	.08	.02	.10	.03	.04	.05	.04	.03	.05	.05	.67
M	.01	.04	.06	.09	.05	.04	.04	.05	.03	.07	.04	.03	.03	.09	.04	.06	.02	.05	.05	.08	.05	.04	.02	

*L = Long condition; S = Short condition; M = Mean across condition

TABLE 5.6

Means for Relative Social Sedentary Behavior By Condition* and Duration Interval

	1	2	3	4	5	6	7	8	9	10	11	12	13	14	15	16	17	18	19	20	21	22	23	M
L	.18	.26	.17	.20	.28	.32	.47	.31	.33	.24	.25	.25	.12	.33	.40	.36	.28	.18	.10	.21	.13	.44	.44	.26
S	.47	.21	.20	.23	.22	.14	.20	.29	.31	.39	.35	.29	.25	.13	.24	.31	.30	.27	.26	.23	.33	.41	.41	.27
M	.33	.24	.19	.22	.25	.23	.31	.30	.32	.31	.30	.27	.19	.23	.33	.34	.29	.22	.18	.22	.23	.43	.43	

*L = Long condition; S = Short condition; M = Mean across condition

The final set of analyses were calculated to determine relati[on] between children's behaviors on the playground at recess and cla[ss-]room behavior immediately following recess. To this end, Pears[on] product correlation coefficients were calculated between aspects [of] playground behavior and measures of classroom fidgeting and co[n-]centration. The results suggest a positive relation exists betwee[n] both social and nonsocial measures of exercise play and fidgeting i[n] class, $r = .15$ and $.13$, respectively. Regarding sedentary behavior[,] social sedentary behavior was positively correlated with concentration, $r = .14$, and negatively correlated with fidgeting, $r = -.17$; nonsocial sedentary behavior was negatively correlated with concentration, $r = -.16$.

Discussion

The general intent of the present study was to examine the extent to which the timing of the recess period effected children's prerecess and postrecess behavior in the classroom, as well as their behavior at recess. More specifically, the effects of confinement time before recess indicated that children, but especially boys, were more restless while doing seat work as a function of time. As time of confinement increased, so did their fidgeting. The prerecess concentration data, while only approaching significance, tell a similar story: concentration on seat work decreased as a function of time. The effects of timing were, however, mediated by gender, at least in the case of fidgeting. Future research should address the extent to which other variables, such as subject matter and classroom structure, interact with periods of confinement, grade level, and gender. We know, for example, that with age girls become less interested in mathematics than boys (Maccoby & Jacklin, 1974). It may be that girls habituate to mathematics seat work in a shorter time than do boys. Such findings could provide important instructional guidance.

These results are consistent with novelty theory, which suggests that children's attention to a task will decrease as a function of time interacting around the tasks. While recess may provide an opportunity for a novel change from seat work, other novel experiences within or outside the classroom may serve a similar function. It may be that social interactive experiences with peers, without a vigorous movement component, may suffice. That gender interacted with condition further suggests that individual difference variables may provide insight into the efficacy of specific treatments. Future research should address the extent to which changes in types of readily addressed. Related specifically to the issue of Novelty Theory, I have examined only one novelty situation: recess; future research should explore other experiences that might be novel for different types of children.

Lastly, I addressed relations between children's behavior at recess and their immediate postrecess classroom behavior. The results indicate that children who engaged in physically active play, such as exercise play, both social and nonsocial, were less attentive when they returned to class. Children who engaged in less vigorous but social activity, on the other hand, were more attentive. These results suggest that recess is doing different things for different children. For some children, typically boys, recess provides an opportunity for physically active social and nonsocial play; for girls, it provides opportunities for less physically active social interaction. Because these data are correlational, they can be interpreted in a number of ways. First, it may be that recess has the "effect" of facilitating boys' physical activity, which in turn results in their restlessness in class. The second, and my preferred, interpretation is that boys are more restless in classrooms than girls, generally. Recess probably does not do much to affect this. The prerecess fidgeting data bore this out: boys, more than girls, fidgeted. Future research should address the extent to which boys and girls are differentially affected by recess duration and types of recess experiences.

On the other hand, that social sedentary behavior at recess is positively related to concentration and negatively related to fidgeting suggests that something important may be going on at recess. Obviously, I cannot make inferences about directionality or "effects" from these correlations but they are insightful on a number of counts. First, the significant relations between recess and classroom behaviors indicate that something "educational" may be going on at recess. The more conservative interpretation of the relations would have children *practicing* at recess those cognitive skills they already possess and use during seat work. Such an interpretation is consistent with the notion of play as practice (Groos, 1901). Indeed, Smith and Hagan use practice theory to explain the effects of confinement on preschoolers' exercise play.

The less conservative interpretation would hold that children on the playground, through social interaction with peers, are *learning* skills that are transferred to the classroom. Such a position is consistent with Piaget's (1970) notions of the facilitative effects of peer interaction on cognition. Of course, my data also indicate that girls more than boys exhibit these social sedentary behaviors. These results may simply mirror that fact that girls, when compared to boys, are more attentive and less restless during classroom seat work.

In summary, the data presented here provide at least a first step in the systematic study of recess, an understudied aspect of the elementary school. The data, again as a first step, suggest that recess is needed and that different levels of confinement have systematic effects. These results have obvious policy and curriculum implications. They also have implications for researchers studying children's playground behavior to the extent that prior confinement and recess duration seem to affect playground behavior. Consequently, caution should be exercised by scholars using more than one sample with different prior confinement periods and recess durations.

Future research in this area is badly needed. For example, studies are needed that minimize observer bias. In the present study, observers were aware of the conditions to which children were assigned as well as the hypotheses. Such knowledge may affect observers' scoring of vague constructs, like attention, vigor, and activity.

Next, multiage studies are needed. We need to know the degree to which recess timing affects children across the primary school period. Does recess play a different role for the kindergarten child than it does for the fourth grader? We know, for example, that boys do different things on the playground at recess as they move across the middle school period and become more concerned with heterosexual relationships (see Chapter 10). They spend less time interacting in same-sex groups and less time in physically vigorous play as they move from year 1 to year 2 of middle school. It seems important to document other age-related changes as children move across the primary school period and their gender roles develop.

References

Baldwin, J., & Baldwin, J. (1978). Reinforcement theories of exploration, play, and psychosocial growth. In E. O. Smith (ed.), *Social play in primates* (pp. 231-253). New York: Academic Press.

Berlyne, D. (1960). *Conflict, arousal, and curiosity.* New York: McGraw-Hill.

————. (1966). Curiosity and exploration. *Science, 153*, 25-33.

Brophy, J., & Putnam, J. (1979). Classroom management in the elementary grades. In D. Duke (ed.), *Classroom management* (pp. 182-216). Chicago: National Association for the Study of Education.

Burghardt, G. (1984). On the origins of play. In P. K. Smith (ed.), *Play in animals and humans* (pp. 5-42). Oxford: Basil Blackwell.

Eaton, W., & Enns, L. (1986). Sex differences in human motor activity. *Psychological Bulletin, 100,* 19-28.

Ellis, M. (1984). Play, novelty, and stimulus seeking. In T. Yawkey and A. D. Pellegrini (eds.), *Child's play* (pp. 203-218). Hillsdale, NJ: Erlbaum.

Fagen, R. (1981). *Animal play behavior.* New York: Oxford: University Press.

Fein, G. (1981). Pretend play: An integrative review. *Child Development, 52,* 1095-1118.

Groos, K. (1901). *The play of man.* London: Heinnemann.

Iowa Test of Basic Skills (1986). Chicago: Riverside Press.

Maccoby, E., & Jacklin, C. (1974). *The psychology of sex differences.* Stanford, CA: Stanford University Press.

Maccoby, E., & Jacklin, C. (1987), Gender segregation in childhood. In H. Reese (ed.), *Advances in child development* (Vol. 6, pp. 239-287). New York: Academic Press.

Martin, P., & Bateson, P. (1986). *Measuring behavior.* London: Cambridge University Press.

Minuchin, P., & Shapiro, E. (1983). The school as a context for social development. In E. Hetherington (ed.), *Handbook of child psychology* (Vol. 4, pp. 197-274). New York: Wiley.

National Association of Elementary School Principals. (1990). *NAESP Principals' Practices Survey: Recess in Your School.* Alexandria, VA: Author.

Piaget, J. (1970). Piaget's theory. In P. Mussen (ed.), *Carmichael's manual of child psychology* (Vol. 1, pp. 703-732). New York: Wiley.

Smith, P. K., & Connolly, K. (1980). *The ecology of preschool behaviour.* London: Cambridge University Press.

Smith, P. K., & Hagan, T. (1980). Effects of deprivation on exercise play in nursery school children. *Animal Behaviour, 28,* 922-928.

Spencer, H. (1898). *The principles of psychology* (Vol. 2). New York: Appleton.

6

Longitudinal Relations between Playground Behavior and Cognition: Explorations in Social Dimensions of Cognition

Introduction

Recently cognitive developmental theory has undergone a clear shift. In years past Piagetian theory, which conceptualized the child as a solitary being making sense out of his or her world through interacting with the physical world, was dominant. According to this theory, only after establishing concepts in the physical world were children able to apply those same concepts to the social world. More recently, the tables have been turned. Children's cognition is now viewed by many, such as advocates of Vygotskiian theory in child psychology and some students of primate "cognition" in ethology, as originating in social interaction. In this chapter I will explore the relations between social interaction and cognition with one group of children. Specifically, I will present longitudinal data on the relations between kindergarten children's social behavior on the playground and measures of first grade peer status and achievement.

Further, in this chapter I will continue to explore the notion of the playground as a context for assessment that was introduced in the preceding chapter. Earlier I argued that the playground may provide an interesting assessment venue for young children because it is cognitively and socially very demanding but at the same time very motivating for children. This combination should lead to children exhibiting higher levels of competence than on traditional achievement tests.

My research was guided by earlier work I conducted that showed that specific types of oral language used by preschoolers with their peers accurately predicted their early literacy status

(Galda, Pellegrini, & Cox, 1989). In other words, what started off as competence in social interaction with peers changed rather dramatically to competence in traditional achievement tasks. Such qualitative transformations in cognition typically occur when children are five to seven years of age (Kagan, 1971; White, 1966). Thus, I chose to examine in this chapter the kindergarten-to-first-grade transition as a period during which relations between social interaction and cognition may be observed. I postulated that specific forms of social interaction for children in this age range, such as peer interaction and adult interaction, should relate differently to aspects of cognition.

The specific interaction measures included were rather molar measures of interaction: peer interaction, adult-directed behavior, and object play. A number of studies have demonstrated that when given free choice in a play environment, children who choose to interact with peers are more sophisticated, on a number of social cognitive measures, than children who chose to interact with adults (e.g., Harper & Huie, 1985; Pellegrini, 1984; Wright, 1980). These findings are consistent with Piagetian (1970) theory, which suggests that the disequilibration characteristic of peer interaction facilitates development whereas the typically unilateral interaction characteristic of adult-child interaction inhibits development. Regarding object play, research by Rubin (1982) suggests that this form of activity is predictive of school-based achievement because of their behavioral similarities; in both object play and school lessons children work independently on goal-oriented projects.

I thought that the playground would be a particularly good place to study this phenomenon because young children put into enjoyable environments, like playgrounds, with their peers typically exhibit high levels of competence (Waters & Sroufe, 1983; Wright, 1980). Consequently, observations conducted in such a highly motivating context should maximize children's exhibition of competence. As I noted in preceding chapters, such playful contexts typically provide an important motivational component in children's learning.

Correspondingly, placing children in such highly motivating, natural situations is also important from an assessment perspective. When children are in highly motivating and demanding situations they exhibit the high levels of competence necessary to participate in those situations. It may be that the often described difference between children's competence as measured in standardized testing situations and their competence as measured in play situations is due to different levels of motivation to exhibit competence. In the former situation youngsters may see little reason to achieve, while in the latter situation achievement may result in sustained play or interaction with a peer.

Another reason for studying the relation between social interaction and cognition on the playground during recess was that it was the only time during the school day when children have a relatively free rein in choosing with whom they interact and the topics of their interaction. Thus, the playground is an excellent venue for sampling varied forms of children's social interactions.

One of my premises in this chapter is that the most accurate assessments of children's social relationships are those that look at children from different perspectives. So, at one level, children's interactions with peers and adults on the playground will be measured by means of behavioral observations. Additionally, children's relationships with peers will be examined from peers' perspectives and from teachers' perspectives. Peers' perceptions are valuable because they provide data predictive of children's social adjustment; for example, sociometrically unpopular children are at risk for antisocial disorders such as juvenile delinquency (Parker & Asher, 1987). Further, teachers' ratings of children's personality disorders are predictive of children's psychiatric disorders (Rutter, 1967; Rutter & Garmezy, 1983).

I was particularly interested in examining the kindergarten-to-first-grade transition because this is a period in children's development when social interaction and play may be particularly important. As I noted above, qualitative changes in children's development characterize this period. Further, and from a policy perspective, the research for this chapter was conceptualized in reaction to a State of Georgia law (since repealed) that required kindergarten children to pass a standardized paper-and-pencil test to be promoted to first grade.

My intent was to show, once again, that standardized achievement and aptitude measures have limited explanatory power for young children. Zigler and Trickett (1978) made this point a number of years ago while arguing against overreliance on standardized measures of cognition, such as IQ tests, and in favor of measures of social competence to measure the impact of early intervention programs. I also hoped to use these analyses to show legislators and Department of Education people in Georgia that their view of children and the ways by which to study them was too limited.

In summary, I was interested in the extent to which social and cognitive dimensions of children's kindergarten experience would predict an aspect of their cognitive status: first-grade achievement.

As part of this venture children's social behavior on the playground were used to predict achievement one year later. It seems particularly important to look at these relations for children at this specific age level because it is a period of major developmental flux. While it makes good theoretical sense for social behaviors of kindergarten children to predict cognitive status one year later, it may not make sense for this to be the case for older children. Thus, data across grade levels were not pooled in the present analyses.

Method

Subjects

All the children studied attended a suburban public elementary school in Athens, GA; they are the same children described in Chapter 4. The kindergarten children, who were part of a larger study, participated in the study for two years. There were a total of 24 children (14 males and 10 females) who participated in the study for two years; they were 5 years old (M = 64 months) at the beginning of the study. Gender differences were not examined because of sample size.

Procedures

Children were observed on their school playground during the recess period from October to May for two years following procedures outlined in Chapter 4. Between 120 and 150 children (from four to five classes at one grade level) were on the playground during each period. There were three to five adults supervising the children.

Each child was observed at least 112 times during each of the two years. Observers recorded the following information (by whispering into a tape recorder) for each scan: the target's name; the location of the playground; the number of boys, girls, and adults in the play group; target's behavior; and reactors' behaviors.

Behaviors noted in the scan sampling included:

1. *Peer Interaction*: socially interactive behavior with peers, such as walking and talking with peers, playing games, and engaging in vigorous physical play, like chase and rough-and-tumble play.
2. *Object Play*: behaviors in which children, playing alone, were manipulating/building with objects, such as building castles or piling stones.

3. *Adult-Directed Behavior*: instances of child-initiated contacts with an adult.

Reliability was established by having observers simultaneously conducting 50 scan samples. To prevent reliability decay, checks and retraining occurred monthly. Reliability was calculated using Cohen's *kappa*; the reliability for the scan samples ranged from .68 to .92 ($M = .80$).

Measures

Some of the measures I used were already described in Chapter 4 and will only be listed here: the popularity, antisocial, and neurotic scores from Rutter's questionnaire. I also used achievement and behavioral measures.

Children's achievement was measured in kindergarten with the Metropolitan Readiness Test (MRT; Nurss & McGauvran, 1976). The MRT has a mean split-half reliability coefficient of .94; its predictive validity is .68 and .72 with the Metropolitan Achievement Test reading and math subtests, respectively. In first grade achievement was measured with the Georgia Criterion Reference Test (GCRT). The GCRT test is a reliable (i.e., KR - 20 of .92) and content-valid achievement test. For both the MRT and GCRT, the composite achievement, standardized scores were analyzed.

The behavioral measures I used included peer interaction, object play, and adult-directed behavior. Relative frequency scores, based on the first 112 scores for each child, were used in the analyses; the relative frequency scores represented the percent of total behavior accounted for by that category.

Results/Discussion

The goal of the research presented in this chapter was to predict children's first-grade achievement as measured by the GCRT with measures of social interaction on the playground at recess. Predictor variables included the following measures, taken during the preceding kindergarten year: object play, peer interaction, and adult-directed behavior. No other predictor variables were included because of the limited sample size. Predictive relations were tested by regressing the predictor variables onto the GCRT score; the MRT score was entered into the equation first as a way of statistically controlling possible continuity in achievement; the behavioral measures were entered next, in unspecified order. This approach was taken so as to statistically control the stability of achievement from year 1 to year 2. Further, such a strategy would inform me as to the predictive value of the measures of social competence, beyond the standardized test variance. In this way I could determine the extent to which the predictor variables of interest, not confounded by previous achievement, accounted for first-grade achievement. The results, which are presented in Table 6.1, suggest that the kindergarten MRT accounted for 34 percent of the variance in first-grade GCRT, while the behavioral measures accounted for an additional 41 percent of the variance; the total model, then, accounted for 75 percent of the variance in first grade achievement.

Most interesting was the fact that kindergarten achievement, while a significant predictor, left more than one-half of the variance in first-grade achievement unexplained. Again, this finding supports the criticisms of Zigler and Trickett (1978), who argue that standardized measures of children's cognition have limited predictive value. Substantially more variance in first-grade achievement is accounted for when children's behavior in a naturalistic, motivating, environment is considered. I should caution, further, that test scores, though limited in their predictive powers, should not be totally disregarded, for they accounted for a statistically significant portion of the variance in first-grade achievement. "Throwing the baby out with the bath water" would limit our understanding of a very complex phenomenon, school achievement.

The most important aspect of the results relates to the developmental nature of the findings. During this period of developmental flux (Kagan, 1971; White, 1966), aspects of children's object play and peer relationships predicted more traditional

TABLE 6.1

Predictive Relations between Kindergartners' MRT and Behavioral Measures and First-Grade Achievement on the GCRT

Control Variable and Behavioral Measures	Step In	R2	B-Value	F	p
Control/MRT	Forced	.34	.32	9.02	.009
Adult-Directed	2nd	.52	−4.03	6.35	.02
Object Play	3rd	.64	1.90	5.43	.03
Peer Interact	4th	.75	.81	6.46	.01

aspects of school achievement. To illustrate, the object play measure was a positive predictor of achievement. This was a measure of children manipulating sticks, logs, and stones on the playground. It should not be surprising that the cognitive demands of such manipulative play should predict performance on a test with a mathematical thinking component; indeed, object play was a positive, and significant predictor of performance on the math portion of the GCRT ($r = .43$, $p < .05$). Such a relation between object manipulation and early numeracy is certainly consistent with Piagetian (1970) theory and the curricular advice of Kamii and DeVries (1978). Both suggest that logicomathematical thought has its developmental roots in object manipulation. However, caution must be exercised when interpreting such a correlation; clearly, more longitudinal research conducted with this specific question in mind is necessary. For example, observers might attend more closely to what children actually say and do during object play. That this level of analysis was not included in the present study is clearly a limitation.

Further, peer interaction was positively related to achievement while adult-directed behaviors was negatively related to achievement. There are at least two ways to interpret these findings. One interpretation is that children who chose to initiate contact with adults, rather than their peers, in a play arena may have lacked the social skills to interact with their peers. The social competence literature indicates that when young children choose to interact with teachers instead of their peers in play-oriented contexts, teachers do most of the work of maintaining interaction (Harper & Huie, 1985; Pellegrini, 1984; Wright, 1980). On the other hand, when children interact with their peers, they must use their own social competence to initiate and sustain interaction (Dodge, Pettit, McClaskey, & Brown, 1986).

The second, and my preferred, interpretation suggests that these results may be due to the special nature of the context of the school playground at recess. In this situation there were over 100 children on the playground, but only three to five adult supervisors. Clearly, the role of the adults here was custodial, not educational. Thus, with such low-quality interaction it is not surprising that a negative relation between adult-directed interaction and achievement was detected. In the present study, when children and adults were together, compared to when children were with peers, children were passive. More specifically, when children were with adults, they were either silent or the adult was talking. The probability of children not talking, compared to adult talking, was observed at a beyond chance level, using the sign test ($p < .01$), when children and adults were together. Thus, when children and adults were together on the playground, adults talked and children listened. On the other hand, when children were in the presence of their peers, their likelihood of talking, compared to not talking, was beyond chance, using the sign test ($p < .01$). Further, there was a positive correlation between amount of talk and achievement ($r = .18$) and a negative correlation between silence and achievement ($r = -.12$). While neither correlation was significant, each was in the predicted direction, which suggests that interaction is positively related to achievement while passivity is negatively related to achievement. In short, the nature of the recess period may have constrained the adult-child relationship. In other, more conducive settings, such as small-group teaching sessions, the relation between adult-directed behavior and achievement may be positive.

This second interpretation of the varying role of adults in children's cognition in different contexts is consistent with extant research. For example, in free play situations adults generally inhibit older preschool children's exhibition of complex forms of play while peers facilitate it (e.g., Dickinson & Moreton, 1991; Pellegrini, 1984). However, in a small-group, teaching context, such as planning an errand or a classification task, adults are much more effective tutors than are peers (Tudge & Rogoff, 1989).

Future research should consider examining more microlevel aspects of these global peer and adult interaction categories. It would be interesting, for example, to determine the extent to which the complexity of interaction varies as a function of group size. It may be, as Humphrey (1976) has suggested, that larger groups facilitate children's use of more complex cognitive strategies, such as transitivity relationships and negotiation strategies. While there is temptation to "fragment" macrolevel social interaction categories, such as peer interaction or adult-directed interaction, in search of specific interaction variables that predict achievement, there are corresponding costs with such a strategy. Rushton, Brainerd, and Pressley (1983) have shown that as one fragments, or examines subcategories of, variables, one increases error variance; this, in turn, has the effect of reducing the likelihood of significant relations. Similarly, when one aggregates, one reduces error and maximizes the likelihood of significant relations. Fragmentation and the corresponding increase in error is accentuated when one has a small sample. Consequently, it seems necessary to use macrolevel variables, as was done in the present study, when working with a limited sample size.

While these results are consistent with both Piagetian (1970) theories and theories stressing the social origins of intelligence (e.g., Humphrey, 1976), they are counter to the research of Entwisle and colleagues (Entwisle, Alexander, Cadigon, & Pallas, 1987), who minimized the predictive value of kindergarten social experiences. This inconsistency may be due to the different ways in which social data were collected in the two studies. In the present study, direct observations of social behavior were made in a context that elicited social competence. In the Entwisle et al. (1987) study, teacher ratings of children's social competence were used. These different data sources often do not converge (Cairns & Cairns, 1986; Smith & Connolly, 1980). This disconcordance may be due to the fact that teacher rating scales tend to identify individual differences among children and children's relative status to their peers, while behavioral measures identify skills, regardless of children's relative status (Cairns & Cairns, 1986). That my first-grade achievement measure assessed individuals' accumulated skills (i.e., mastery of subject matter), not relative standing (i.e., mastery in relation to peers), may be responsible for the predictive power of the behavioral measures in my regression results.

There are clear research implications for these results. The extent to which dimensions of children's social behavior predicts school achievement is provocative. While it is convenient to explain these results in terms of Piaget's cognitive primacy theory, that is, cognition determines social behavior, it would be interesting to follow the opposite tack. It may be that the demands placed on children during social interaction, such as having to please peers with opposing views and figuring out the classroom dominance hierarchy, may *affect* cognition. Recent research in primatology (e.g., Jolly, 1966; Humphrey, 1976) and older work in sociology (e.g., Bernstein, 1960; Durkheim & Mauss, 1903/1966) suggest a social primacy; that is, social relationships determine logicomathematical forms of cognition.

These results also have important policy implications. Predicting children's achievement is a very difficult enterprise. Use single measures, like standardized tests, limits our understanding of a very complex process. Even when tests are reliable predictors of achievement, which they often are not for young children (see Messick, 1983), the picture they draw is limited: the variance accounted for, while statistically significant, is limited.

References

Bernstein, B. (1960). Language and social class. *British Journal of Sociology*, 2, 217-276.

Bronfenbrenner, U. (1979). *The ecology of human development*. Cambridge, MA: Harvard University Press.

Cairns, R., & Cairns, B. (1988). The developmental-interactional view of social behavior: Four issues of adolescent aggression. In D. Olweus, J. Block, & M. Radkye-Yarrow (eds.), *Developmental of antisocial and prosocial behavior: Research, theory, and issues* (pp. 315-342). New York: Academic Press.

Clarke-Stewart, A., & Fein, G. (1983). Early childhood programs. In M. Haith & J.Campos (eds.), *Handbook of child psychology: Vol. 2, Infancy and developmental psychobiology* (pp. 917-1000). New York: Wiley.

Coie, J., & Dodge, K. (1983). Continuities and changes in children's social status: A five-year longitudinal study. *Merrill-Palmer Quarterly, 29*, 261-287.

Coie, J., Dodge, K., & Coppotelli, H. (1982). Dimensions and types of social status: A cross-age perspective. *Developmental Psychology, 18*, 557-570.

Dickinson, D., & Moreton, J. (1991, April). *Predicting specific kindergarten literacy skills from three-year-olds' preschool experiences*. Paper presented at the biennial meetings of the Society for Research in Child Development, Seattle.

Dodge, K., Pettit, G., McClaskey, & Brown, M. (1986). Social competence in children. *Monographs of the Society for Research in Child Development, 5(2)*.

Durkheim, E., & Mauss, M. (1903/1966). De quelques formes primitives de classifications. In M. Mauss (ed.), *Oeuvres* (Vol. 2). Paris: Editions de minuit.

Entwisle, D. (1990). School and the adolescent. In S. Feldman & G. Elliot (eds.), *At the threshold* (pp. 197-224). Cambridge, MA: Harvard University Press.

Entwisle, D., Alexander, K., Cadigan, D., & Pallas, A. (1986). The schooling process in the first grade: Two samples a decade apart. *American Educational Research Journal, 23*, 587-613.

————. (1987). Kindergarten experience: Cognitive effects or socialization. *American Educational Research Journal, 24*, 337-364.

Epstein, J. (1989). Family structures and student motivation. In C. Ames & R. Ames (eds.), *Research on motivation in education* (pp. 259-295). San Diego, CA: Academic Press.

————. (in press). School and family partnerships. In *Encyclopedia of Educational Research*.

Galda, L., Pellegrini, A. D., & Cox, S. (1989). A short-term longitudinal study of preschoolers' emergent literacy. *Research in the Teaching of English, 23*, 292-310.

Harper, L., & Huie, K. (1985). The effects of prior group experience, age, and familiarity on the quality and organization of social relations. *Child Development, 56*, 704-717.

Haywood, G., Rothenberg, M., & Beasley, R. (1974). Children's play and urban playground environments: A comparison of traditionally, contemporary, and adventure types. *Environment and Behavior, 6*, 131-168.

Humphrey, N. (1976). The social function of intellect. In P. Bateson & R. Hinde (eds.), *Growing points in ethology* (pp. 303-317). Cambridge: Cambridge University Press.

Jolly, A. (1966). Lemur social behavior and primate intelligence. *Science, 153*, 501-506.

Kagan, J. (1971). *Continuity and change in infancy.* New York: Wiley.

Kamii, C., & DeVries, R. (1978). *Physical knowledge in preschool education.* Engelwood Cliffs, NJ: Prentice-Hall.

Lykken, D. (1968). Statistical significance in psychological research. *Psychological Bulletin, 70*, 151-159.

Martin, P., & Bateson, P. (1988). *Measuring behavior.* London: Cambridge University Press.

Messick, S. (1983). Assessment of children. In W. Kessen (ed.), *Handbook of child psychology: Vol. 1, History, theory, and methods* (pp. 477-526). New York: Wiley.

Nurss, J., & McGauvran, M. (1976). *The Metropolitan Readiness Test.* New York: Harcourt Brace Jovanovich.

Ogbu, J. (1988). Culture, development, and education. In A. D. Pellegrini (ed.), *Psychological basis of early education* (pp. 245-276). Chichester, UK: Wiley.

Parker, J., & Asher, S. (1987). Peer relations and later personal adjustment: Are low-accepted children at-risk? *Psychological Bulletin, 102*, 357-389.

Pellegrini, A. (1984). The social-cognitive ecology of preschool classrooms. *International Journal of Behavioral Development, 7*, 321-332.

Piaget, J. (1970). Piaget's theory. In P. Mussen (ed.), *Carmichael's manual of child psychology* (Vol. 1, pp. 703-732). New York: Wiley.

Rubin, K. (1982). Nonsocial play in preschoolers: Necessary evil? *Child Development, 53*, 651-657.

Rushton, J., Brainerd, C., & Pressley, M. (1983). Behavioral development and construct validity: The principle of aggregation. *Psychological Bulletin, 94*, 18-35.

Rutter, M. (1967). A children's behavioral questionnaire for completion by teachers. *Journal of Child Psychology and Psychiatry, 8*, 1-11.

Rutter, M., & Garmezy, N. (1983). Developmental psychopathology. In E. M. Hetherington (ed.), *Handbook of child psychology: Vol. 4, Socialization, personality, and social development* (pp. 775-912). New York: Wiley.

Smith, P. K., & Connolly, K. (1980). *The ecology of preschool behaviour*. London: Cambridge University Press.

Spodek, B. (1985). Kindergarten. In T. Husen & T. Postlethwaite (eds.), *International encyclopedia of education* (pp. 2812-2814). New York: Pergamon Press.

Tudge, J., & Rogoff, B. (1989). Peer influences on cognitive development: Piagetian and Vygotsian perspectives. In M. Bornstein & J. Bruner (eds.), *Interaction in human development* (pp. 17-40). Hillsdale, NJ: Erlbaum.

Waters, E., & Sroufe, L. (1983). Social competence as a developmental construct. *Developmental Review, 3*, 79-97.

White, S. (1966). Evidence for a hierarchical arrangement of learning processes. In L. Lipsett & C. Spiker (eds.), *Advances in child development and behavior* (Vol. 2). New York: Academic Press.

Wright, M. (1980). Measuring the social competence of preschool children. *Canadian Journal of Behavioral Science, 12*, 17-32.

Zigler, E., & Trickett, P. (1978). I.Q., social competence, and evaluation of early childhood intervention programs. *American Psychologist, 33*, 789-798.

7

The Rough-and-Tumble Play of Primary School Children: Contemporaneous and Longitudinal Relations

The research I will present in this chapter covers the study of rough-and-tumble play (R&T) through the primary school grades. As I noted in previous chapters, R&T is an important component of children's playground behavior. The chapter is organized such that R&T is first defined, especially in relation to aggression. Then age and gender differences are presented in terms of the frequency with which it is observed on the school playground. Next, I will address the functional consequences of R&T at different points in ontogeny.

What is R&T?

Researchers in both the child developmental (Smith & Vollstedt, 1985) and the animal (Fagen, 1981) literatures have great difficulty in defining "play." The problem does not get any easier when one attempts to define a specific aspect of play, in this case, R&T. To minimize difficulties, researchers define play along a number of different dimensions such as those displayed in Figure 7.1. Ethologists often define play according to behaviors, affect, consequence, and structure. Defining R&T according to *behavioral* dimensions, it can be described as a physically vigorous set of behaviors, such as hit at, jump on, run after, chase, and play fight. *Affectively*, R&T can be characterized by positive affect and a play face. R&T can also be defined according to *consequence*, or those behaviors that follow it; socially affiliative behaviors such as games often follow R&T. From a *structural*, or *role*, perspective, R&T can be defined as reciprocal to the extent that children typically alternate between subordinant roles, such as being chased or being the victim, and superordinant roles, such as chasing or being the victimizer.

There are also other, less commonly used criteria by which R&T

FIGURE 7.1

R&T and Aggression

	R&T	Aggression
Behaviors	Vigorous	Vigorous
	Soft contact	Hard contact
	Locomotive	
Affect	Play face	Scowl/Frown
Consequence	Affiliation	Separation
Roles	Reciprocal	Unilateral
Ecology	Outdoors/Spacious	Property disputes
	Soft areas	
Development	Inverted-U function	Flat
Gender	Boys > Girls	Boys > Girls

can be defined. They include: the ecology of occurrence, age-related changes, and gender-related patterns. *Ecologically*, we know that R&T is more likely to occur in spacious areas than in confined areas (Smith & Connolly, 1980). Also, it often occurs in dramatic play areas (Pellegrini, 1984); the fantasy play themes of boys in particular often have physically vigorous components, such as superhero characters. R&T is frequently observed on playgrounds. As I noted earlier, R&T is more likely to occur on those parts of the playground that have soft, grassy surfaces. The reason is obvious: children are less likely to hurt themselves in these areas than on harder surfaces.

Age is another dimension along which R&T can be defined. Play generally follows an inverted-U developmental function (Fagen, 1981; Rubin, Fein, & Vandenberg, 1983). Extant R&T data and the data to be presented in this and later chapters support this conclusion. R&T accounts for about 5 percent of preschool children's play behavior (Humphreys & Smith, 1984), about 10-15 percent during the late childhood period, and then drops down to about 5 percent again during adolescence. As an aside, the co-occurrence of R&T and fantasy during the preschool period may be partially responsible for the reported low frequency of occurrence R&T. Researchers concerned with preschoolers' play, if given the choice, would probably code a fantasy R&T bout as fantasy, rather than R&T.

Gender differences in R&T are robust: boys engage in more R&T than do girls. This is probably due to both hormonal and socialization events. Male hormones and stereotyped treatment of boys combine to make this a clearly observed difference throughout childhood and adolescence.

An important aspect of defining R&T involves comparing it with aggression, a form of behavior with which it is often confused. Aggression is defined along the same dimensions as R&T to explicate their differences; these dimensions are also displayed in Figure 7.1. *Behaviorally*, aggression is characterized by closed-hand, not open-hand hits, and by hard, not soft, contacts. *Structurally*, aggression is characterized by unilateral, not reciprocal, roles; aggressors do not readily offer to switch places with their victims. Correspondingly, a *consequence* of aggression is that one of the children, usually the victim, tries to separate from the other. *Affectively*, aggression is marked by negative affect and scowl/frown.

Aggression and R&T are also distinct along other dimensions. *Ecologically*, aggression usually occurs in the context of property disputes; it is not more likely to happen in any one section of the playground. Like R&T, however, aggression follows *gender* typing such that boys more than girls are aggressive. The extent to which aggression varies with *age* is also different from R&T: the curve for aggression is stable from childhood through adolescence (Olweus, 1976). So, along traditional dimensions, R&T and aggression are distinct. In the course of this chapter the distinction between aggression and R&T will be made repeatedly. While in most cases during childhood they are distinct, in other cases they are not.

Study 1

Descriptions of Age and Gender Trends

The data reported in this section represent my first observational work on the topic of R&T. My motivation for studying R&T were numerous. First, I was fascinated with the ethological methods used to study R&T. As I noted in Chapter 3, this approach seems to be a fruitful one to follow for child developmentalists. Second, R&T seemed to be a natural extension of my interests in preschool children's fantasy play. Indeed, in some of my descriptive work in this area Jane Perlmutter and I found that R&T did co-occur with fantasy (Pellegrini & Perlmutter, 1987). Most of the research in the area of R&T had been done with preschool children in the United Kingdom. After a stay in Sheffield with Peter K. Smith, one of the "founding fathers" of the study of children's R&T, I was convinced that a descriptive, empirical base for R&T during the primary school period was needed. As I noted above, if R&T resembled other forms of play, one would have expected its frequency of occurrence to increase during this period. Relatedly, if children spent more time engaging in R&T, one would also expect its functional importance to increase. That is, there should be a relation between the resources that one expends while playing, such as caloric output and possible risk of injury, and benefits, such as social skills learning. Thus, the intent of the first series of observations was to document age-related trends in relative frequency of R&T and the extent to which R&T related to aspects of social competence.

Method

The participants in this study have been described in Chapters 4 and 6. Briefly, boys and girls in grades K, 2, and 4 were observed at least 100 times on the school playground across the school year. Children's R&T and aggression were also event sampled.

Also as described above, children's sociometric status was assessed following techniques outlined by Coie and Dodge (1983); social impact and social preference scores were derived from this procedure. Children's social problem solving was also assessed following the work of Spivak and Shure (1974) whereby the variety of children's responses to hypothetical social problems was scored. Teachers completed a behavior questionnaire designed by Rutter (1967) for each child; this questionnaire yielded an antisocial factor score. Lastly, children viewed a series of 10 videotaped bouts that were either aggression or R&T; they were scored in terms of the number of correct interpretations.

Results/Discussion

The first cut of the data involved grade (3: K, 2, and 4) × gender (2) ANOVAs on relative frequencies of R&T and aggression. While no significant variation by grade was observed for R&T or aggression, they both varied by gender with boys (16 and .30 percent, respectively) exhibiting more R&T and aggression than girls (7 and .20 percent, respectively). Further, R&T and aggression were not significantly intercorrelated for either boys ($r = -.13$) or for girls ($r = .01$).

That aggression did not vary by grade level is not surprising to the extent that aggression is a stable phenomenon across childhood (Olweus, 1976). I expected R&T to vary across this period, however. That it did not may have been due to my limited sample size in that the incidence of R&T did increase, although not significantly, from kindergarten to second grade, and then declined at fourth grade.

That boys engaged in R&T and aggression at higher rates than girls is not surprising. This is a robust finding in both the child development and animal literatures. Hormonal and socialization events in the history of boys and girls guarantee such differences. Regarding hormonal events, male hormones, such as androgen, have an organizational effect on the brain and the nervous system and subsequent play behavior of lower animals, such as rats, and higher primates, such as humans (Ehrhardt, 1984; Meyer-Bahlburg, Feldman, Cohen, & Ehrhardt, 1988). The most convincing child-related data come from natural experiments involving pregnancy difficulties in which mothers take male hormones for treatment (Meyer-Bahlburg et al., 1988). While controlling for alternate explanations, such as pregnancy difficulties, it was found that *both* male and female children exposed to male hormones in utero, exhibited more "hypomasculine" behavior, such as R&T, between the ages of eight and fourteen. Thus, male hormones seem to predispose boys to this form of vigorous behavior.

This propensity for boys to engage in vigorous and rough physical behavior is readily re-enforced by most levels of society. As infants, male children engage, more than females, in R&T bouts, primarily with their fathers (MacDonald, 1993). Further, the types of toys that boys receive as preschoolers, such as balls and toy guns (Huston, 1983), are conducive to rough and physical play. The vigorous nature of boys' play, in turn, predisposes them to prefer the outdoors, over indoors, as a play area (Harper & Sanders, 1975) and other boys as playmates (Maccoby, 1986). This gender-related preference for outdoors and vigorous play, as we will see later, continues until early adolescence. These biological and social factors, then, come together to predispose boys to R&T.

Given this pervasive gender effect on R&T, the obvious question to be posed next is, what does it mean? As I noted earlier in this chapter, ethological theory presupposes a cost-benefit explanation. That is, behaviors that are "expensive," or that require large amounts of energy (i.e., caloric expenditure) and/or are dangerous (e.g., regarding possibility of injury) should have a corresponding benefit. The ethological literature provides further guidance in the search for theoretically consistent outcomes of R&T. Generally, we should look for similarities in design features between R&T and outcome measures. For example, R&T is characterized by vigorous behavior, reciprocal role taking, and peer affiliation; consequently, similar features should characterize outcome measures, such as vigorous reciprocal games and peer affiliation measures like popularity. Similarly, if R&T is conceptualized as an aggressive construct, it should be related to other forms of aggression and antisocial behavior.

To this end I calculated correlations between R&T and aggression and outcome measures, separately by gender; they are displayed in Table 7.1.

TABLE 7.1

Correlations Between R&T Relative Frequency and Social Competence

	R&T		Aggression	
	Boys	Girls	Boys	Girls
Social preference	.36**	−.18	−.05	.01
Soc prob solv flex	.31*	.14	.16	.22
Discrim R&T/aggress	.21	.17	−.32	.00
Antisocial factor	.02	.36**	.01	.01

$*p < .05$ $**p < .01$

As the table indicates, girls' R&T was not significantly correlated with measures of social competence. This is consistent with the cost-benefit model discussed above: girls spend little time in R&T and therefore they probably do not accrue many benefits. Girls' R&T did, however, relate to teachers' ratings of them as antisocial. This may be a case of gender stereotyping such that girls who engage in male activities are perceived to be antisocial.

Boys' R&T was positively related to social preference and social problem solving and led to higher participation in cooperative games at a beyond chance probability. The relation between R&T and social preference was expected in light of it being an affiliative activity. It seems particularly important for boys to engage in R&T with someone they know well and regard as a friend, given the possibility that such play could easily be misinterpreted and lead to aggression. There is less possibility of R&T leading to aggression among children who are popular because these children are less aggressive.

The correlation between R&T and social problem solving may have been due to the "flexibility" dimension of play. Specifically, numerous theorists suggest that play is flexible to the extent that children are divergent and attend to means, rather than ends, during play (Bruner, 1976; Sutton-Smith, 1968). This argument suggests that the flexibility learned or nurtured during play should generalize to other aspects of development. This was the theoretical motivation for Sutton-Smth's (1968) original formulation for the relation between play and creativity and the subsequent empirical work on play and creativity and problem solving carried out by Dansky and Silverman (1976, 1978) and Sylva, Bruner, and Genova (1976), respectively. Clearly the present results do not specifically test this flexibility hypothesis in that the flexibility dimensions of R&T per se was not measured, but the results are consistent with that hypothesis. Data specific to the flexibility hypothesis will be presented later in this chapter.

Another way in which to examine relations between R&T and measures of social competence is to examine the temporal consequences of R&T. That is, what behaviors followed the termination of an R&T bout? If R&T served an aggressive function, one would expect it to be followed by aggression at a reliable rate. If, on the other hand, it related to other aspects of reciprocal role taking one would expect it to be followed by other forms of vigorous reciprocal interaction, like cooperative games. Separate 2-state sequential analyses were conducted examining the probability of R&T going to games and of R&T going to aggression. R&T went to games, like tag, at a greater than chance probability, whereas the R&T to aggression probability was not greater than chance. Again, R&T and aggression do not seem to be related at this age. R&T may lead to cooperative games because it, as in games like tag, involves children chasing each other and alternating roles. In summary, R&T seems to be a gender-specific construct. Primary school boys seem to accrue benefits from R&T in terms of social skills/social competence learning.

Study 2

Study 1 suggested that there may be a relationship between age and R&T. While the decrement in R&T described above was not significant, the primate play literature does suggest that R&T should decline in frequency as children progress through childhood. Thus, in Study 2 a group of older boys was studied. Also in this study, the construct R&T was "unpacked" so that I could determine the contribution made to social competence by specific components of R&T. This is particularly important for a multidimensional construct like R&T. It contains numerous dimensions, some of which are not unique to play per se (such as positive affect and reciprocal role taking).

In this second study two specific dimensions of R&T were considered: flexibility and vigor. As I noted above, the flexibility hypothesis of play has been advanced for a number of years. To my knowledge, however, it has not been empirically tested. That is, researchers have not observed flexibility dimensions of play and then related them to relevant outcome measures. The flexibility hypothesis of R&T would be supported if this dimension of R&T related to flexibility in social problem solving. The level of vigor, or roughness, of R&T is also relevant to social competence. Maccoby (1987) suggests that this is an important component in peer affiliation generally, and in gender segregation specifically, to the extent that girls avoid playing with boys because the latter are too rough. Correspondingly, boys may choose to affiliate with each other because they enjoy such types of play. Vigor of play, then, may be an important component in one aspect of boys' affiliative network: social preference.

Moreover, Study 2 addressed a critical and persistent problem in play research: the problem of equifinality. The problem of equifinality states that organisms can reach specific ends via different developmental paths (Martin & Caro, 1985). With reference to R&T, some boys may become socially competent by means other than R&T. To understand equifinality clearly, take the case of girls: they become socially competent despite their usual lack of interest in R&T play. They utilize other forms of reciprocal social interaction to learn and practice necessary social skills for social problem solving and popularity. Some boys may also use other avenues. In short, a developmental outcome is often reached via very different routes.

In this study the equifinality issue was addressed by first controlling variance in measures of social competence (i.e., social preference and social problem solving) related to *non-R&T* forms of reciprocal social interaction in hierarchic regression formulas. Second, relative frequency of R&T as a macrolevel variable was also entered into the equation as a control so that I could determine the extent to which specific aspects of R&T related to social competence. Third, specific aspects of R&T (vigor and flexibility) were entered into the aggression formulas. If these last variables accounted for a significant portion of the variance in social competence, we could with confidence state that these variable were the important aspects in R&T for these aspects of social competence.

In this study the nature of the sample was different than that used in Study 1. A sample consisting entirely of older boys was drawn. That only boys were studied follows from the earlier results suggesting that they, not girls, accrued benefits form R&T. Older boys were the particular subjects of study because I wanted to examine the extent to which the role of R&T changed with age. The primate literature suggest that as animals move from childhood to adolescence, and the frequency with which they engage in rough play decreases, those who continue to engage in this form of play may be using it for aggressive or dominance exhibition ends. Unlike the rough play of younger boys, the rough play of early adolescent boys may be used to show off, to exhibit dominance, or as a way of aggressing against a peer.

I chose two ways to test this dominance/aggression hypothesis. The first was to correlate R&T to peer-nominated dominance status. The second was to examine the dominance symmetry of boys' R&T groups. In this process the extent to which the focal boys had a dominance status higher, lower, or equal to the others in the R&T group was examined. I assumed that if boys consistently chose to engage in R&T with boys of lower dominance status, they could be using those bouts to reinforce dominance. Relatedly, if they chose to play with boys of equal or greater status, I assumed that they were using R&T to establish dominance.

Method

Subjects and procedures. Boys were drawn from the same elementary school as the samples reported above. The 37 boys had a mean age of 11½ years. Observational procedures used followed focal child sampling/continuous recording rules; each child was sampled once per week across a 20-week period . During each 3-minute focal sample boys' behaviors were described. Theoretically relevant behavioral categories included: R&T (with 10 behavioral components); cooperative games; and other forms of reciprocal social interaction, such as talking, pushing on a swing, and so on. Additionally, focal children's playmates were identified as well as the number of children in the immediate group.

Measures. I employed four behavioral measures. *Flexibility of R&T* was operationalized in terms of the number of different components of R&T (1-10) a boy exhibited: tease, hit and kick at, chase, poke, pounce, sneak-up, carry child, pile on, play fight, hold and push. *Vigor of R&T* was defined along a 7-point continuum, following Maccoby and Jacklin (1987). *Reciprocal social interaction* was any sedentary social interaction that was reciprocal. *Group size* was determined by the number of children in the immediate vicinity of the focal boy.

I also used three child interview measures. In these cases individual children were interviewed by an experimenter. *Social problem-solving flexibility* was defined as in earlier studies reported, however, boys' negative and positive solutions were separated. Boys' *dominance* was assessed, following Sluckin and Smith (1977), as part of the sociometric interview, by having them nominate the "toughest" boys in the class; boys received a rank-order score. *Popularity* was defined, as noted in earlier chapters, by having individual children nominate, from an array of individually pictured classmates, three children they "liked most" and three they "liked least." The unit of analysis was social preference, or "Likes Most-Least."

Results/Discussion

The analysis strategy utilized was a very conservative one. That is, in determining the role of specific dimensions of R&T on social competence, a hierarchic regression strategy was used such that two other variables (reciprocal social interaction and relative frequency of R&T) were entered before R&T vigor or flexibility. In this way the specific impact of these dimensions of R&T, independent of other rival factors, could be determined. Specifically, by entering other forms of social interaction first into the equation, the equifinality issue is addressed by determining its contribution to social competence. By entering relative frequency of R&T next the variance in that measure which is correlated with, but not unique to, R&T vigor and flexibility can then be controlled.

In the first analysis boys' prosocial and antisocial solutions to hypothetical social problems were examined. The regression model, displayed in Table 7.2, for both measures tell a similar story. Neither control variable was significant, but variety of R&T behaviors was a significant predictor. This result is certainly consistent with the flexibility hypothesis of play, but it may be the case that variety of behavioral categories is what is important. It may be that variety represents one's behavioral repertoire and the more varied the repertoire, the more competent one is. It would also be interesting to examine other aspects of variety and flexibility. The aspect of variety chosen here was rather simpleminded. Other more interesting measures might include the variety of behavioral sequences used in R&T. This is certainly an area that merits further study.

In the second analysis, social preference was the criterion variable and R&T/vigor was entered into the regression model after the control variables. This model too is displayed in Table 7.2. While both reciprocal social interaction and relative frequency of R&T account for significant in social preference, vigor does not.

These results are interesting for at least two reasons. First, the vigor dimension of R&T was not important, possibly because extreme vigor may be both rare in schools and not very attractive to

TABLE 7.2

Hierarchic Regression Models for
Social Problem Solving and Social Preference

Variable	Order Entered	B-Value	R2	p
Social Problem Solving –				
Reciprocal	1	.98	.09	.31
R&T/%	2	−.61	.09	.56
R&T/Vigor	3	1.39	.32	.001
Social Problem Solving +				
Reciprocal	1	3.67	.05	.32
R&T/%	2	3.11	.05	.31
R&T/Variety	3	3.30	.22	.006
Social Preference				
Reciprocal	1	.04	.07	.03
R&T/%	2	−.87	.14	.14
R&T/Vigor	3	.09	.15	.59

a majority of potential playmates. The other interesting aspect of this regression model was that while the relative frequency of R&T was significantly related to social preference, it was a negative correlation. That is, high rates of R&T meant low levels of social preference. This negative correlation between R&T and social preference may have been due to the fact that sociometrically defined popular and rejected boys engage in R&T at near equal rates; thus the negative relation could be due to the inclusion of rejected boys. This issue will be addressed in greater depth in my summary of Study 3. The negative relations may also have been due to the age of this group of boys. That they were in early adolescence supports the findings in the primate literature where rough play is used for dominance exhibition and aggressive ends.

To test this dominance hypothesis more directly, the symmetry of boys' peer groups in R&T, social games, and other forms of reciprocal social interaction was examined. To this end, the dominance status of the focal boys (as determined by his mean class rank) was compared to other children with whom he initiated interaction. In each of the different forms of social interaction, boys' groups were symmetrical beyond chance. Thus, they did not choose less dominant boys for R&T partners. Boys probably choose to interact with others of like dominance status so as to minimize exploitation and the possibility of aggression.

Study 3

In Study 3 the extent to which children's sociometric status effected the forms and functions of their R&T was examined. Specifically, the R&T of popular and rejected children, both boys and girls, was examined in the context of both contemporaneous and longitudinal research designs. Because of the sample demands of sorting children into these sociometric categories, the studies of primary school popular and rejected children all confound sociometric group with gender.

Popular and rejected children are different in many ways. By definition, popular children are liked by more people than are rejected children. While children can be rejected for numerous reasons, aggression is a persistent predictor of childhood rejection (Coie & Dodge, 1983). It has also been suggested that popular and rejected children process social information differently. Dodge and associates (e.g., Dodge & Frame, 1982) have amassed impressive research data demonstrating the social information processing deficits of rejected children and the relation between this deficit and subsequent aggression. So, for example, when popular and rejected boys view or take part in an ambiguous social provocation bout, such as R&T, members of the former group of boys should be able to process information more accurately than members of the latter group. This deficit, in turn, relates to their attributing aggressive intent to such events. In other words, rejected children tend to interpret an R&T bout as aggressive, while popular children tend to interpret it as playful.

While popular and rejected children are different on a number of factors, they are alike in one interesting way. At the primary school level, they engage in R&T at the same rates, about 8 percent of total behavior (Coie & Kupersmidt, 1983). That these very different children engage in R&T at similar rates may be responsible for the observed negative correlation between R&T and social preference. It may be that rejected boys engage in R&T and that escalates into aggression because rejected boys do not adequately processes ambiguous social information. Thus in this third study I examined the different ways in which popular and rejected children interpreted R&T bouts. This was accomplished by showing videotaped bouts of R&T and aggression and asking children to discriminate between the two; they were then asked to list as many reasons as they could to justify their answers. The social-information-processing-deficit hypothesis would suggest that rejected, compared to popular, children would have poorer discrimination and give fewer attributes.

Children's meaning for behaviors such as R&T can also be inferred behaviorally. Ethologists accomplish this task typically by factor analyzing behaviors and assigning meaning to co-occurring behaviors and by examining the consequences of target behaviors. I followed a similar strategy in my third study. R&T and aggressive behaviors were factor analyzed separately for popular and rejected children; when R&T and aggression co-occur the category is aggressive. Additionally, the extent to which R&T was followed by aggression or cooperative games should also help determine the extent to which it is an aggressive or affiliative behavior.

In addition, popular and rejected children's R&T was related to their ability to solve hypothetical social problems of the sort described earlier, and also to the extent to which they were considered antisocial by their teachers. If children's R&T and aggression co-occurs, as might be the case for rejected children, we would not expect it to correlate with social problem-solving flexibility simply because it is not flexibility: it would be characterized by unilateral, not reciprocal and varied, roles. Similarly, if R&T is aggressive, as may be the case for rejected but not popular children, teachers should consider the former group antisocial.

In short, in this study I explored the extent to which different types of children assign different meaning to a set of seemingly similar behaviors. This was accomplished, first, by asking children about R&T and aggressive bouts. In contrast to this rather emic tack, a more etic approach was also used in factor analyzing R&T and aggressive behaviors. To extend our understanding of the ways in which children assign meaning to behaviors, the consequences of R&T were examined both longitudinally across a two-year span and immediately following R&T bouts. Such an approach allowed me to begin to make inferences about the function of R&T for these different sorts of children.

Methods

The children in this study were the same as those participating in Study 1 and all procedures followed were similar to those described above. The only additions concerned the way in which popular and rejected children were defined and a description of the films they viewed. Children's sociometric status was determined by following procedures outlined by Coie and colleagues (1982) such that popular children had standardized social preference scores greater than zero, and standardized "likes most" and "likes least" scores of greater than and less than zero, respectively. There were a total of 26 popular children from grades K, 2, and 4 (11 boys, 15 girls). Rejected children were those with standardized social preference scores of less than −1 and a "likes most" standardized score of less than zero. There were 16 rejected children (11 boys, 5 girls). Children were studied from the beginning of year 1 to the end of year 2.

During year 1 all children viewed 11 bouts that were either R&T or aggression. They were asked concerning each bout: Is this play fighting or real fighting? Why do you think so? All responses were tape-recorded. The first bout was a practice item and the remaining 10 were scored as correct/incorrect and the variety of attributes given per child for each type of bout was also scored.

Children were observed on the playground during both years. Of specific interest to this study were three observational categories: aggression, R&T, and cooperative games. R&T was defined along the same 10 dimensions as outlined in Study 2 and aggression was categorized along two dimensions: insult and hit with closed hand. Children's cooperative, social, and rule-governed games were defined as reciprocal social interaction, such as tag, catch, follow the leader, and hide 'n' seek.

Also in both years, children solved hypothetical social problems and their teachers completed Rutter's antisocial questionnaire.

Results/Discussion

The first analyses were separate factor analyses conducted on the year 1 behavioral dimensions of R&T and aggression for popular and rejected children. These analyses should be cautiously interpreted in light of the small sample in relation to the number of variables analyzed. The principal components' factor structures are displayed in Table 7.3; only factor scores of > .4 are displayed. As can be seen, the factor structures for popular and rejected boys are very different. For popular children one factor seems to represent a playful provocation factor (poking and teasing); this factor may represent an initial phase of R&T used to elicit playful responses. The second factor is more like a play-fighting factor (kick at, push, play fight, and chase) described by Harlow (1962) many years ago. In both cases, these types of R&T behaviors, when they involve popular children, result in continued affiliation. Specifically, in sequential lag analyses, the R&T of popular children led to cooperative games at a greater than chance probability; it did not lead to aggression. Thus R&T for popular children of the age is a cooperative and affiliative construct, not an aggressive one.

TABLE 7.3

Factor Pattern of R&T and Aggression for Popular and Rejected

Behavior	Popular		Rejected	
	Factor 1	Factor 2	Factor 1	Factor 2
Closed-hand hit			.86	
Tease		.94	.60	−.50
Kick at	.68			
Poke		.83		
Pounce			.83	
Play fight	.73		.89	
Chase	.69		.85	
Hold			.46	
Push	.74		.50	.50
Hit at			.95	

The R&T of rejected children is very different. First, R&T and aggressive behaviors co-occurred in the factor analyses. Relatedly, the year 1 R&T of rejected children led sequentially to aggression at a higher than chance probability when the R&T to aggression transitional probabilities were tested; it did not lead to affiliation. Thus, behavioral analyses led to the conclusion that the R&T of rejected children is aggressive, not cooperative, while the R&T of popular children is cooperative.

These conclusions are supported by subsequent analyses. For example, teachers' ratings of antisocial personality on Rutter's scale was significantly correlated ($r = .47, p < .06$) with R&T for rejected children. The correlation for popular children was negative ($r = -.30$). Thus, the correlation data suggest that during year 1 R&T for rejected children was aggressive and antisocial, while for popular children it was cooperative and not aggressive.

By way of explanation, rejected children's R&T may be aggressive for numerous reasons. As I noted above, the information-processing-deficit hypothesis suggests that rejected children process less information and attribute aggressive intent to ambiguous provocation events. The year 1 data corroborate this: rejected children were significantly less accurate in discriminating R&T and aggression than were popular children. Further, popular children, compared to rejected children, listed significantly more attributes for R&T (e.g., They aren't really hitting; They're laughing) and aggression (e.g., He's trying to get away; There's a bunch of kids watching).

Rejected children may turn R&T into aggression because they do not possess a varied social problem-solving repertoire. When presented with a social problem they may resort to aggression as a default solution. Popular children, on the other hand, may have a more varied repertoire. This repertoire is correlated with their R&T. It may be that their R&T helps them learn more varied strategies or is a practice place for already acquired strategies. In either case, R&T is valuable for popular children's social competence but not for the competence of rejected children. In order to tease out some of the directional and developmental issues a longitudinal design is necessary.

The strengths of a longitudinal design are that they permit us to make antecedent-consequence statements and also allow us to control statistically the year-to-year stability of the criterion variables. Specifically, with the longitudinal data predictive role of R&T in cooperative games and social problem solving flexibility were examined. In this design the year 1 measures of games and social problem solving were statistically controlled so that their temporal stability and intercorrelation with R&T during year 1 does not account for the predictive relation. Without such control a relation between year 1 R&T and year 2 games could be due to the fact that during year 1 R&T and games are intercorrelated and that the year 1 to year 2 correlations between R&T and games is really due to the temporal stability of games. By controlling year 1 games, the unique contribution of year 1 R&T to year 2 games can be determined. In short, an important alternate hypothesis is controlled.

The year-to-year relation are displayed in Table 7.4. Regarding year 1 R&T predicting year 2 cooperative games, while controlling year 1 games, a significant relation was observed for popular but not for rejected children. Second, year 1 R&T for popular children also predicted year 2 social problem-solving flexibility but did not do so for rejected children. These results replicate and extend the contemporaneous results in that both data sets show the R&T of popular children moving into games and both data sets show that R&T predicts social problem solving.

The longitudinal data are also interesting to the extent that they enable us to begin to eliminate alternate hypotheses. In this case the year-to-year correlation is not due to stability of games or social problem solving. Indeed, the year-to-year correlation of games was not significant for either group yet their social problem solving was stable.

TABLE 7.4

Regression for Longitudinal Relations for Popular and Rejected Children

	Variable	Order	R2	F	p
	Games				
Rejected	Yr 1 Games	1	.005	.04	.9
	Yr 1 R&T	2	.006	.01	.9
Popular	Yr 1 Games	1	.02	1.28	.27
	Yr 1 R&T	2	.21	4.18	.05
	Social Problem Solving Variety				
Rejected	Yr 1 Prob Solv	1	.58	9.59	.01
	Yr 1 R&T	2	.59	.01	.9
Popular	Yr 1 Prob Solv	1	.15	3.23	.11
	Yr 1 R&T	2	.28	3.02	.09

Conclusion

To conclude, R&T seems to mean very different things to different children. For popular children, it is a playful and cooperative activity that is a reasonable predictor of important aspects of social competence such as cooperative game playing and social problem solving. In light of the nonhuman primate R&T literature, we can assume that R&T for popular children does serve a social competence function. They seem to use and practice a varied social repertoire that positively predicts social flexibility and cooperative social interaction.

The R&T of rejected children is a very different story. R&T for them is aggressive, not cooperative. Correspondingly, they do not accrue the benefits form R&T that popular children do. The data presented here support the social-information-deficit hypothesis. An alternate hypothesis, put forth by Smith (1989), suggests that the R&T to aggression transition may be intentional, not accidental. The idea here is that children's aggression is tied to their securing some resource, such as dominance status. In order for this theory to be supported, we would have to see evidence that the information processing capabilities of these children is not deficient. Further, they should pick peers to engage in R&T whom they can reliably dominant or bully. The data for primary school children do not support this hypothesis. In Chapter 10 I will outline the way in which this changes when individuals move from childhood into adolescence.

References

Bernt, T., & Hoyle, S. (1985). Stability and change in childhood and adolescent friendships. *Developmental Psychology, 21,* 1002-1015.

Billman, J., & McDevitt, S. (1980). Convergence of parent and observer ratings of temperament with observations of peer interaction in nursery school. *Child Development, 51,* 395-400.

Blurton Jones, N. (t972). Categories of child interaction. In N. Blurton Jones (ed.), *Ethological studies of child behavior.* (pp. 97-129). London: Cambridge University Press.

Bruner, J. (1972). The nature and uses of immaturity. *American Psychologist, 27,* 687-708.

Coie, J., & Dodge, K. (1983). Continuities and changes in children's social status: A five-year longitudinal study. *Merrill-Palmer Quarterly, 29,* 261-282.

———— . (1986). Hostile and instrumentally aggressive children: A social information processing perspective. Paper presented at the Annual Meeting of the American Psychological Association, Washington, DC.

Coie, J., Dodge, K., & Coppotelli, H. (1982). Dimensions and types of social status: A cross-age perspective. *Developmental Psychology, 18,* 557-570.

Dodge, K., & Frame, C. (1982). Social cognitive biases and deficits in aggressive boys. *Child Development, 53,* 620-635.

Eaton, W., & Enns, L. (1986). Sex differences in human motor activity. *Psychological Bulletin, 100,* 19-28.

Fagen, R. (1984). Play and behavioral flexibility. In P. K. Smith (ed.), *Play in animals and humans* (pp. 159-174). London: Basil Blackwell.

———— . (1981). *Animal play behavior.* New York: Oxford University Press.

Hinde, R. (1982). *Ethology.* London: Fontana.

Humphreys, A., & Smith, P. K. (1984). Rough-and-tumble in preschool and playground. In P. K. Smith (ed.), *Play in animals and humans* (pp. 241-270). London: Blackwell.

———— . (1987). Rough-and-tumble play, friendship and dominance in school children: Evidence for continuity and change with age. *Child Development, 58,* 201-212.

Ladd, G. (1983). Social networks of popular, average, and rejected children in school settings. *Merrill-Palmer Quarterly, 29,* 283-307.

Lenerz, K., Kincher, J., Lerner, J., & Lerner, R. (1986). Contextual demands for early adolescent behavioral style. *Journal of Early Adolescence, 6,* 279-291.

Maccoby, E. (1986). Social groupings in childhood. Their relationship to prosocial and antisocial behavior in boys and girls. In D. Olweus, J. Block, and M. RadyeYarrow (eds.), *Development of antisocial and prosocial behavior: Research. theory, and issues* (pp. 263-280). New York: Academic.

Maccoby, E., & Jacklin, C. (1987). Gender segregation in childhood. In H. Reese (ed.), *Advances in child development* (Vol. 20, pp. 239-287).

Martin, P., & Bateson, P. (1986). *Measuring behaviour.* London: Cambridge University Press.

Martin, P., & Caro, T. (1985). On the functions of play and its role in behavioral development. In J. Rosenblatt, C. Beer, M. C. Bushel, & P. Slater (eds.), *Advances in the study of behavior* (Vol. 15, pp. 59-103). New York: Academic.

Pellegrini, A. D. (1988). Elementary school children's rough-and-tumble play and social competence. *Developmental Psychology, 24,* 802-806.

———. (1989). Elementary school children's rough-and-tumble play. *Early Childhood Research Quarterly, 4,* 245-260.

———. (1991). *The rough-and-tumble play of adolescent boys of differing sociometric status.* Poster presented at the British Psychological Society-Developmental Section-Meetings. Cambridge, September.

Routh, D., Schoeden, C., & O'Trama, L. (1979). Development of activity levels in children. *Developmental Psychology, 10,* 163-168 .

Rubin, K., Fein, G., & Vandenberg, B. (1983). Play. In E. M. Hetherington (ed.), *Handbook of child psychology* (Vol. 4, pp. 693-779). New York: Wiley.

Sackett, G., Sameroff, A., Cairns, R., & Suomi, S. (1981). Continuity in behavioral development: Theoretical and empirical issues. In K. Immelmann, G. Barrow, L. Petrinovich, & M. Main (eds.), *Behavioral Development* (pp. 23-57). New York: Cambridge University Press.

Savin-Williams, R. (1979). Dominance hierarchies in groups of early adolescence. *Child Development, 50,* 142-151.

Sluckin, A., & Smith, P. K. (1977). Two approaches to the concept of dominance in preschool children. *Child Development, 48,* 917-923.

Smith, P. K. (1982). Does play matter? Functional and evolutionary aspects of animal and human play. *The Behavioral and Brain Sciences, 5,* 139-184.

—— . (1989). The role of rough-and-tumble play in the development of social competence: Theoretical perspectives and empirical evidence. In B. Schneider, G. Attili, J. Nadel, & R. Weissberg (eds.), *Social competence in developmental perspectives* (pp. 239-255). Hingham, MA: Kluwer Academic Publishers Group.

Spivak, G., & Shure, M. (1979). *Social adjustment of young children.* San Francisco: Jossey-Bass.

Sutton-Smith, B. (1968). Novel responses to toys. *Merrill-Palmer Quarterly, 14,* 151-158.

Thomas, A., & Chess, S. (1977). *Temperament and development.* New York: Brunner/Mazel.

Windle, M., Hooker, K., Lerner, K., East, P., Lerner, J., & Lerner, R. (1986). Temperament, perceived competence, and depression in early and late adolescence. *Developmental Psychology, 22,* 384-392.

Windle, M., & Lerner, R. (1985). *Revised Dimensions of Temperament Survey-Child (Self).*

—— . (1986). Reassessing the Dimensions of Temperamental Individuality Across the Life Span: The Revised Dimensions of Temperament Survey (DOTS-R). *Journal of Adolescent Research, 1,* 213-220.

8

Preference for Outdoor Play during Early Adolescence

Introduction

In the preceding chapters I discussed what elementary school children do on the school playground at recess. These behaviors should be interpreted within a framework in which the recess period was mandatory. That is, all children had to go outdoors for recess unless the weather was inclement or they were ill. Thus, this situation represents a natural experiment of sorts to the extent that, in such situations, we as researchers can omit an important confound: children's self-selection to specific environments confounding the effects of the recess period or the playground environments.

I have also discussed in earlier chapters how this mandatory recess period was a methodological convenience for researchers to the extent that it minimized a self-selection confound. While convenience for researchers is certainly not in the foreground for educational policymakers, mandatory recess is very inconvenient for studying other related aspects of recess and outdoor play, such as children's preference for choosing to play outdoors or indoors.

Studying children's choice of outdoor or indoor recess can be conceptualized in terms of what they choose to do with their leisure time. Leisure, or free-time, activities in school settings can provide valuable information on children's peer culture and socialization. Children's entry into and passage through middle school presents a particularly interesting opportunity to study children's choice of activities and peer groups. They, as early adolescents, are entering a new institution at a time when they are simultaneously spending more time with peers in school and less time with peers in their neighborhoods and less time with members of their families; consequently, children's choices regarding middle school-based activities and peer groups represent important points in the social development of early adolescents (Brown, 1990).

Young adolescents differ reliably from younger children in their choices of free-time activities. Most notable are the gender differences between the childhood and adolescent periods. Children's preference to spend free time indoors or outdoors seems to be a particularly important choice marker. As I noted in Chapter 2, during the preschool period boys, more than girls, prefer to play outdoors (Harper & Sanders, 1975). Relatedly, there are reliable gender differences in levels of physically vigorous play from infancy through adolescence: boys' play is much more vigorous than girls' play (Eaton & Enns, 1986). Boys' preference to play outdoors is probably related to their preference for vigorous play. That is, outdoor play spaces, compared to indoor play spaces, are typically more spacious; more space per child is, in turn, positively related to vigorous play (Smith & Connolly, 1980). These results are often interpreted as supporting the hypothesis that boys, more than girls, have a biological bias toward "outdoorishness" (Money & Ehrhardt, 1972; Ehrhardt, 1984). Outdoor behavior of adolescents in schools has not been thoroughly studied, primarily because school make little or no provision for such activities. Further, where it has been studied, it has been studied sociologically (Lever, 1976), and no effort was made to test the sociobiological hypothesis beyond the preschool period.

The composition of the affiliative groups in which children spend their free time also differs systematically by gender. In terms of size of peer group, boys congregate in larger, more extensive peer groups than do girls. This finding has been reported for children from the preschool period (Hartup, 1983) through adolescence (Fine, Mortimer, & Roberts, 1990). That boys tend to congregate in public places and girls in private places (Fine et al., 1990) may also be related to the outdoor/indoor choice issue to the extent that outdoor places also tend to be more public than indoor spaces.

Another dimension of affiliative groups, gender composition, also differs systematically by gender: boys and girls from the preschool period to the beginning of adolescence tend to interact in gender-segregated groups (Hartup, 1983). With the onset of adolescence, peer groups become more integrated in terms of gender (Brown, 1990).

This literature allows us to conjure a picture of the ways in which children spend their free time in school, living in gender-segregated worlds where boys spend time in large groups running around the playground while girls interact in small groups in more private, typically indoor, places. This picture, while relatively complete for children in preschool settings, is incomplete at the point when young adolescents enter middle school. In the present chapter, the picture for young adolescents just entering middle school will be extended at both the descriptive and the explanatory levels.

At the descriptive level, behavioral studies of boys' and girls' preference for outdoor/indoor play are limited to the preschool period (Harper & Sanders, 1975). Studies of older children's indoor/outdoor preference have utilized questionnaires (e.g., Garton & Pratt, 1987) or self-report methodologies (e.g., Kleiber, Larsen, & Csikszentmihalyi, 1986). This may be due to the fact that older children are not given many opportunities for leisure, or recess, periods during school time.

Where older children do have recess periods, direct observations of their choice to play outdoors would provide an interesting comparison with the previously reported methodologies, which have well-known limitations, such as reactivity. Further, direct observations would allow us to determine the actual duration of children's outdoor play, the behaviors they exhibit, and the social groups in which they occur. The study of early adolescents' activity choice as they begin and progress through middle school would be particularly interesting from a developmental perspective to the extent that it would provide information on the stability of gender differences for outdoorishness, vigorous activity, and gender segregation as children make the transition to adolescence. The peer groups formed on the playground at recess time continue, during the early adolescence period, at least through sixth grade, to be an important aspect of children's peer culture, only to wane as children pass through the end of the middle school period, with seventh and eight grades (Brown, 1990).

Entry into middle school begins a period in which children's social relationships, and their corresponding choice of some free-time activities, should remain stable while others should undergo change. Questionnaire-based data (Garton & Pratt, 1987) led to the hypothesis that boys, more than girls, continue to prefer outdoor play and should play outdoors for longer periods because of their continuing interest in sports. Sports, such as basketball and football, are often played outdoors at recess by middle school boys (Pellegrini, 1991). Further, this preference should not change during the middle school period because of the important place of sports in adolescent boys' lives (Fine et al., 1990). The first objective of my research with middle school children was to examine the effects of grade level and gender on children's preference for and duration of outdoor play.

The second objective of my research was to proffer an explanation for these hypothesized gender differences in preference for the outdoors. Currently little data exist to explain why children choose indoors as opposed to outdoors. As I noted above, one level of explanation derives from a biosocial perspective according to which boys' preference for the outdoors and vigorous play are determined by a biological predisposition for such environments (Ehrhardt, 1984). Correspondingly, boys' play groups may be segregated by gender because they enjoy rough activities while girls do not (Maccoby, 1986). Consequently, a bias for outdoorishness exists for boys but not for girls.

In this study I explored some of the possible biosocial correlates of preference for outdoor activity. I chose temperament as a proxy for youngsters' biological predisposiiton for physical activity. This choice was based on two facts. First, the physical activity dimension of temperament is considered to have a biological/hormonal component and it is stable from childhood through adolescence. That is not to say that biology, at birth, predisposes children to certain temperamental categories. It does suggest that specific biological processes are implicated in temperament and that these are stable. The second reason for choosing temperament was convenience: other more direct measures, such as hormonal assays, were unobtainable for this study.

As alluded to above, there are also psychological/behavioral explanations—for example, sex role preference for outdoors/indoors—and sociological explanations—for example, teacher attitudes toward boys and girls playing outdoors—for children's choice to spend free time outdoors. At the behavioral level, children, typically boys, who engage in rough, vigorous play should prefer to spend time outdoors while those who engage in more social sedentary activities, typically girls, should spend less time outdoors.

Correspondingly, children who are considered good at games should prefer outdoors because that is where these skills can be exhibited for their peers to observe. Many of the games played on the middle school playground, however, are rough and therefore involve children exhibiting physical dominance over their peers (Pellegrini, 1991). If these dominance-related behaviors were observed in large peer groups of boys, the dominance exhibition explanation for choosing outdoor play would be supported. The strategy utilized for the second objective of this study was to factor analyze theoretically relevant measures of adolescents during the first two years of middle school. The measures included temperament/activity, number of female and male peers observed with focal subjects on the playground, total number of peers in the group, dominance status, passive and rough social behavior, and frequency of times observed outdoors.

I expected male peers in large groups, activity, frequency outdoors, and dominance to co-occur as a factor indicating "outdoorishness." I also expected female peers, passive interaction, and small numbers in groups to co-occur, reflecting more sedentary, female-preferred social activity.

In addition, teachers rated children in terms of their achievement, facility in games, and physical attractiveness. These items should reflect teachers' positive or negative attributions of children. I expected variation on these items to be indicators of children's accommodation to the institutional demands of the school.

These factor analyses should provide some level of explanation for children's choice to play outdoors. Another reason for choosing factor analyses techniques is that they have been used in previous questionnaire research on adolescents' preference for indoor/outdoor play (Garton & Pratt, 1987; Kleiber et al., 1986). Consequently, by keeping analytic techniques similar, comparisons between questionnaire and observational methods could be made.

It is also interesting from a developmental perspective to determine the extent to which these gender-segregated and dominance-related factor patterns persisted across children's middle school experience. My third objective was to examine the effects of grade and gender on these factors. Do they change or do they remain the same with grade level? I expected change as adolescents become more interested in heterosexual relationships.

Method

Subjects

The site of this study was a rural public school in the northern part of the state of Georgia. The total sixth and seventh grades of the middle school were recruited for the research. However, only children whose parents' consented to their participation in the study were included. The grade span of the middle school was grades 6 through 8. The total population of these grades was 138 in the sixth grade (73 males and 65 females) and 167 in the seventh grade (83 males and 84 females), for a total of 305. The racial composition of the school was overwhelmingly Caucasian: only 11 out of 305 students were black, Hispanic, or Asian. To avoid a racial confound, only Caucasian children were included in the study. A sample of 133 children (71 sixth graders, with 36 males and 35 females and a mean age of 12.4 years; 62 seventh graders, with 32 males and 30 females and a mean age of 13.8 years) was identified.

Procedures

There were two outdoor periods available daily. One period was in the early morning and the other after lunch; each lasted between 15 and 20 minutes. Children were free either to go outdoors or to stay indoors during recess. Children who stayed indoors could sit in their rooms and talk with friends and/or walk around the corridors. Children who chose to go outdoors spent their time in the school courtyard located in the middle of numerous school buildings and bordering asphalt walkways. The grassy courtyard area was of rectangular shape, measuring approximately 25 meters × 35 meters.

There were two observers of children's behavior. The observers were also teachers in the school so their presence was unobtrusive. The observers did not conduct any of the interviews with the children nor were they aware of the children's status on the measures to be described. Observations followed focal child sampling and continuous recording rules (Martin & Bateson, 1986). Specifically, focal children were observed, in counterbalanced order, for 3-minute periods. Their behavior was recorded continuously for 3 minutes or until the children were out of sight for 30 seconds. Observers stayed close enough to focal children so that they could clearly see facial expressions and hear their language. Observers recorded children's behavior, identified the children with whom the focal child was interacting, and the location of the child; all this was done by talking into small portable tape recorders. Observations began at the start of the recess period. Data presented here are taken from children who were observed a minimum of 10 times across the school year. The mean number of observations across the sample was 31.32. The order in which children were observed was counterbalanced.

The mutually exclusive category system of children's playground behavior was based on the extant work of Humphreys and Smith (1987) and Pellegrini (1988). The full category system has nine molar categories, each of which had molecular components. (see Chapter 4 for the details on all nine categories.) In the present study two behavioral categories were analyzed:

Passive/interactive: talk to/talked at by adult; talk to/talked at by
    peer; give/receive comfort; groom/groomed; dress/dressed;
    offer/receive/refuse object.
Rough games: play face; run with/without ball; stand with ball;
    watch in game; throw/catch ball; block/is blocked; tackle/is tack-
    led.

Additional information coded while children were being
observed included:

Group size: the number of children in the focal child's immediate
    vicinity at the start of the recording.
Gender of playmates: the gender of the individual children compris-
    ing the immediate group described above.
Number of observations: the frequency of separate focal samples
    conducted on each child outdoors.
Duration of observations: the number of 5-second intervals per
    observation, that is, the relative frequency of 5-second intervals
    for all observations for each subject.

Reliability checks were made at two levels. First, reliability
checks were made on the accuracy of the verbal encoding of focal
children's behavior. This was accomplished by having two observers
simultaneously encoding the behavior of the same focal child. The
two regular observers, as well as a third observer, conducted checks
on 25 percent of the focal child samples. Comparisons of two tape
recordings per sample were made. The level of agreement between
the observers across the 25 percent was .83 (*kappa*). The second
level of reliability involved checking the accuracy of the assignment
of the verbal encodings into the categories described above. This was
accomplished by randomly choosing 25 percent of the focal sample
tapes and having a trained coder (someone not involved in the observations) recording them. The level of agreement was .91 (*kappa*).

Measures

Children's dominance was assessed following the method used
by Humphreys and Smith (1987), and described by me in earlier
chapters. Individual child's rating was the mean rating across the
whole class.

Children's homeroom teachers were given two questionnaires,
Coie and Dodge's Teacher Checklist (n.d.) and Keough's Measure of
Temperament (1982), for each child in January of the school year.

They were told to read over the questionnaires, but not to complete them. In this way they could familiarize themselves with the questionnaire items in relation to the target children. In April, they were asked to complete them. The two teachers who acted as observers did not observe the children for whom they completed questionnaires. Descriptions of each of the two teacher questionnaires follow.

Coie and Dodge's Teacher Checklist (n.d.) has 45 items, each scored from 1 (low) to 5 (high). Four of these items were analyzed in this study: the items dealing with the child's physical attractiveness, his or her ability in games, and a collapsed score of their math and reading achievement level.

Keogh's (1982) Measure of Temperament has 23 items which the teacher rate from 1 through 5. The items (i.e., items #1, 2, 9, 10, 17) for the physical activity component of temperament were used because they provide information on children's level of physical activity (e.g., child has difficulty sitting still).

Results/Discussion

My first objective was to determine the effects of grade and gender on children's choice of outdoor free time and the duration of their stay outdoors. For the number of times subjects were observed outdoors per observation a grade (2:6 and 7) × gender (2) analysis of variance (ANOVA) was calculated on the frequency of observations outdoors. Post hoc comparison were made according to the Student Newman-Keuls procedure with a .05 *alpha*. A significant gender effect was observed, $F(1,117) = 7.56$, $p < .006$, as was a significant gender × grade interaction, $F(1,117) = 25.47$, $p < .0001$. Boys ($M = 38.22$, $SD = 27.31$) went out more than girls ($M = 24.48$, $SD = 19.19$). In the sixth grade, boys ($M = 48.36$, $SD = 19.42$) went out significantly more than girls ($M = 10.33$, $SD = 4.35$); there were no significant gender differences in seventh grade (boys, $M = 27.42$, $SD = 20.77$, girls, $M = 28.63$, $SD = 19.21$). Further, sixth grade boys went out significantly more than seventh grade boys.

Next, the duration of children's stay outdoors was examined. To this end, the effects of grade and gender on the average duration of each child's stay outdoors was determined with a 2 × 2 ANOVA; the dependent measure was the number of 5-second intervals per observation. Significant grade, $F(1,87) = 12.16$, $p < .0008$, and gender, $F(1,87) = 11.73$, $p < .001$, effects were observed. Sixth graders ($M = 138.69$, $SD = 110.53$) spent longer sustained periods outdoors than seventh graders (M = 90.02, SD = .66.96), and boys (M = 137.67, SD = 107.45) were outdoors for longer periods than girls (M = 96.05, SD = 57.83).

Next, factor analyses were conducted to determine the extent to which theoretically relevant variables formed reliable factors. The variables chosen were: teacher ratings of physical attractiveness; teacher ratings of games skills; teacher ratings of temperament/activity; teacher ratings of achievement; social/passive interaction on the playground; rough games on playground; number of peers in playground groups; male peers in playground groups; females peers in playground group; frequency of times observed on playground; peer ranking of dominance. Principal components analysis procedures, with a varimax rotation, were utilized and factors were limited to those with eigenvalues greater than 1.0. Loadings of .35 and above were considered necessary for inclusion in a factor. Three factors emerged. The factor structure is displayed in Table 8.1.

The factors were labeled: Teachers' Choice, Active Female Oriented, Outdoor Male Oriented. They each accounted for the following amounts of variance: 2.40, 2.17, and 1.64, respectively. Notable in the factor structures is the overlap of rough social play and number of peers in both factors two and three. Both factors are characterized by rough behavior, while the positive and negative values assigned to number of peers indicates different ends of a continuum.

TABLE 8.1

Factor Pattern

	Teachers' Choice	Active Female-Oriented	Outdoor Male-Oriented
Attractive	0.73		
Good at games	0.67		
Poor student	0.64		
Active		0.46	
Female peers		0.60	
Passive social behavior		−0.79	
Rough social behavior		0.70	0.49
Number peers		−0.55	0.57
Dominance			0.52
Male peers			0.75
Frequency outdoors			0.78

The third objective was to examine the extent to which these three factors varied by children's grade and gender. To this end, separate grade (2) × gender (2) ANOVAs were calculated for each factor; dependent measures were the separate factor scores resultant from the above reported factor scores. For the Teachers' Choice factor, only a significant effect for grade was observed, $F(1,132) = 6.82, p < .01$; sixth graders ($M = .20, SD = .04$) were rated higher than seventh graders ($M = -.25, SD = .02$).

For the Active Female Oriented factor, significant effects for grade, $F(1,132) = 46.69, p < .0001$, and gender effects, $F(1,132) = 4.10, p < .04$, were observed; seventh graders ($M = .13, SD = .01$) exhibited higher levels than sixth graders ($M = -.10, SD = .005$) and girls ($M = .46, SD = .13$) more than boys ($M = -.56, SD = .29$).

For the Outdoor Male Oriented factor, significant main effects for gender, $F(1,132) = 19.81, p < .0001$, and grade, $F(1,132) = 8.37, p < .004$, were observed; additionally, a significant gender × grade interaction was observed, $F(1,132) = 6.26, p < .01$. Boys ($M = .39, SD = .31$) exhibited more than girls ($M = -.32$) and sixth graders ($M = .17$) more of this factor than seventh graders ($M = -.21, SD = .09$). The interaction revealed that sixth grade boys ($M = .79, SD = .36$) exhibited more Outdoor Male Oriented behavior than seventh grade boys ($M = -.05, SD = .002$); no other between-group comparisons were significant.

The first objective was to examine the extent to which boys, compared to girls, preference for outdoor activity continued into early adolescence. Extant research with preschool children demonstrates reliable gender differences (Harper & Sanders, 1975). The results from the present study suggest that this gender difference exists when children first enter middle school, in the sixth grade, but does not continue through seventh grade. Further, the younger children, of both genders, and boys spent longer periods outdoors when they chose to go out.

An explanation for these diminishing gender differences may be that as children enter and begin to move through an institution like middle school, their identity changes from children to adolescents. For children, gender segregated groups are appropriate. For adolescents, with the emerging interest in heterosexual relationships, they are becoming more interested in integration than segregation. Thus, as they move through middle school, they self-select themselves less frequently into such a stereotyped environment as the outdoors. That there were no *explicit* institutional policy differences regarding sixth and seventh graders' outdoor time leads me to minimize grade differences due to specific school effects.

Individual schools, however, are sometimes different and the possibility of age differences being due to school policy, either implicit or explicit, must not be ignored. That my research was conducted in only one school obviously limits its generalizability and leaves open the possibility of specific school effects. Future research utilizing more than one school will be needed to test the generalizability of these results.

My results are inconsistent with those studies utilizing questionnaire methodology (Garten & Cartmel, 1986; Garten & Pratt, 1987), which found gender differences in adolescents' leisure preference and activity choice. The differences may be due to methodological differences (i.e., observation vs. questionnaire), nationality differences (i.e., American vs. Australian), age differences in the samples (high school vs. middle school students), or to differences between specific schools. Future research should address directly comparisons between observational and questionnaire methodologies as well as specific school effects. Use of a longitudinal design, within one school, could address the grade differences without the possible school effect confound.

My second and third objectives were to examine the factor structure of measures related to children's outdoor play and how these factors varied by grade and gender, respectively. The first factor is composed of measures that were all completed by teachers. This factor represents children whom teachers consider physically attractive, not doing well in math and reading, and good at games. The absence of outdoor play as an element in this factor, both sedentary and rough, suggest that these children chose to spend their leisure time indoors rather than outdoors.

This factor varied only by grade, with younger children being rated higher than older children. A life course (Entwisle, 1990) interpretation to adolescence is one possible way to explain these data. This approach emphasizes the interaction between individuals, as adolescents, and their transitions into school environments. Research following the life course approach has shown that as children enter middle school or junior high school they experience low levels of achievement; this changes as they progress through and accommodate to the institution and their new status as adolescents (Entwisle, 1990). Further, the younger children may have been viewed more positively by their teachers than the older children because the former group may have accommodated to teachers' rule systems as they made the transition into a new and unsettling school environment.

The second factor, which was more frequently observed for girls than for boys, is typified by relatively small female peer groups (indicated by the negative loading of Number of Peers and positive loading of Female Peers) that exhibit both rough and socially active behavior (indicated by the positive loading of Rough Social Behavior and negative loading of Passive Social Behavior, respectively) when they are on the playground. Further, teachers consider these children to be temperamentally active. That frequency of play outdoors did not load on this factor suggests further that these children did not choose to go outdoors frequently, but when they did go out they were active. This group seems to be composed of "high energy" girls who chose to go outdoors only when they were feeling particularly active, which does not seem to be that often. The grade effect for this factor may indicate that as these "active" girls felt comfortable being in middle school, they more freely expressed their propensity toward activity.

The third factor is characterized by boys who exhibit rough behavior in large groups. These boys are considered by their peers to be dominant, or "tough," and frequently choose to play outdoors. This group seems to be composed of children who choose to engage in rough behavior outdoors to exhibit dominance. The gender × grade level interaction on this factor indicated that the gender differences existed only to the extent that sixth grade boys exhibited more rough behavior than all other children; no significant gender differences were observed at seventh grade. These results too can be explained by life course theory. Specifically, we know that adolescence is a time when children's peer groups and their status in these groups (Brown, 1990; Entwisile, 1990) are being reformulated.

More specific to boys' peer groups, adolescence is a time when their dominance status in groups is in flux (Fagen, 1981; Pellegrini, 1991; Zakriski & Wright, 1991). Dominance status during the period of early adolescence moves from a physically, aggressive basis to a more affiliative base (Zakriski & Wright, 1991). The sixth grade boys in the present study were new to the middle school at a time when they were also in this transitional phase of peer/dominance relationships. As a way of trying to establish their dominance in a new situation they relied on exhibitions of quasi-aggression, or rough play. As they became socialized to the school setting, in seventh grade, this reliance on rough play and dominance declined.

In conclusion, boys' preference for the outdoors and rough play in early adolescence marks a transition point. The outdoorishness and rough play that characterizes the behaviors of younger children changes as children become adolescents and enter middle school.

There are also clear limitations in this study that should be addressed in future research. First, I advocate a combination of biological and more psychological orientations. In the present study a measure of children's temperament was used as a biological proxy. Temperament, while it has a biological component and evidences stability across childhood, is an indirect measure. More direct measures of biological processes, such as hormonal assays, measures of heart rate, and skin conductivity should be gathered in the future. This advice, however, must be tempered by the realism of conducting research in schools where school policy and parental concerns may prohibit such intrusive techniques.

The second limitation has been noted already, and that relates to the use of only one school. At the most general level, more schools would be nice to test the generalizability of these results; a replication sample design of the sort used by Smith and Connolly (1980) would be appropriate. At a more specific level, the use of more than one school in the sample would help determine the extent to which the grade differences I observed were due to school differences or to the psychological processes of early adolescence.

Also, as I suggested above, a longitudinal study of children as they progress through middle school would be the ideal, from a developmental perspective, way in which to study change across grades, without a specific school confound. In the next chapter, these data are framed in a longitudinal design.

References

Boulton, M., & Smith, P. K. (1990). Affective bias in children's perceptions of dominance relationships. *Child Development, 61,* 221-229.

Brown, B. B. (1990). Peer groups and peer cultures. In S. Feldman & G. Elliot (eds.), *At the threshold* (pp. 171-196). Cambridge, MA: Harvard University Press.

Eaton, W., & Enns, L. (1986). Sex differences in human motor activity. *Psychological Bulletin, 100,* 19-28.

Ehrhardt, A. (1984). Gender differences: A biosocial perspective. In S. Sondergegger (ed.), *Nebraska Symposium on Motivation* (pp. 37-57). Lincoln:University of Nebraska Press.

Entwisile, D. (1990). School and the adolescent. In S. Feldman & G. Elliot (eds.), *At the threshold* (pp. 197-224). Cambridge, MA: Harvard University Press.

Fagen, R. (1981). *Animal play behavior*. New York: Oxford University Press.

Fine, G., Mortimer, J., & Roberts, D. (1990). Leisure, work, and the mass media. In S. Feldman & G. Elliot (eds.), *At the threshold* (pp. 225-252). Cambridge, MA: Harvard University Press.

Garton, A., & Cartmel, A. (1986). Adolescent leisure pusuits and interests in the 1980's: Some sex and age difference. *Australian Educational and Developmental Psychologies, 3*, 5-11.

Garton, A., & Pratt, C. (1987). Participation and interest in leisure activities by adolescent school children. *Journal of Adolescence, 10*, 341-351.

Goldsmith, H., Buss, A., Plomin, R., Rothbart, M., Thomas, A., Chess, S., Hinde, R., & McCall, R. (1987). Roundtable: What is temperament? Four approaches. *Child Development, 58*, 505-529.

Harper, L., & Sanders, K. (1975). Preschool children's use of space: Sex differences in outdoor play. *Developmental Psychology, 11*, 119.

Humphreys, A., & Smith, P. K. (1987). Rough-and-tumble-play, friendship, and dominance in school children: Evidence for continuity and change with age. *Child Development, 58*, 201-212.

Keogh, B. (1982). Children's temperament and teacher decisions. In R. Porter & G. Collins (eds.), *Temperamental differences in infants and young children* (pp. 267-278). London: Pitman.

Kleiber, D., Larson, R., & Csikszentmihalyi, M. (1986). The experience of leisure in adolescence. *Journal of Leisure Studies, 18*, 169-176.

Lever, J. (1976). Sex differences in games children play. *Social Problems, 23*, 479-487.

Maccoby, E. (1986). Social groupings in childhood. In D. Olweus, J. Block, & M. Radye-Yarrow (eds.), *The development of antisocial and prosocial behavior* (pp. 263-284). New York: Academic Press.

Martin, P., & Bateson, P. (1986). *Measuring behaviour*. London: Cambridge University Press.

Money, J., & Ehrhardt, A. (1972). *Man & woman, boy & girl*. Baltimore: Johns Hopkins University Press.

Pellegrini, A. (1988). Rough-and-tumble play and social competence. *Developmental Psychology, 24*, 802-806.

———. (1991, September). *Rough-and-tumble play of adolescent boys of differing sociometric status*. Paper presented at the annual meetings of the British Psychological Society, Developmental Section. Cambridge, United Kingdom.

Savin-Williams, R. (1979). Dominance hierarchies in groups of early adolescents. *Child Development, 52*, 142-151.

Smith, P. K. (1989). The role of rough-and-tumble play in the development of social competence. In B. Schneider, J. Nadel, & R. Weissberg (eds.), *Social competence in developmental perspective* (pp. 239-255). Hingham, MA: Kluwer.

Smith, P. K., & Boulton, M. (in press). Rough-and-tumble-play, aggression, and dominance. *Human Development*.

Smith, P. K., & Connolly, K. (1980). *The ecology of preschool behavior.* London: Cambridge University Press.

Spivak, G., & Shure, M. (1974). *Social adjustment of young children.* San Francisco: Jossey-Bass.

Zakriski, A., & Wright, J. (1991, April). *Perceptions of dominance in children's peer groups: Age differences in the relation between aggression, status, and dominance.* Poster presented at the biennial meetings of the Society for Research in Child Development, Seattle.

9

Longitudinal Relations between Social Networks and Adjustment to Middle School

Introduction

Entering a new school is a major event in the lives of students and their families. In the best of circumstances, students' lives are changed, or disrupted, to the extent that in these new institutions students typically experience a different set of rules governing academic work and their social behavior with peers and adults (Davies, 1982). For example, students' academic work in secondary school, compared to primary schools, may be less closely scrutinized due to their having numerous teachers, not just one teacher, in the course of the school day. Socially, middle schools and junior high schools, when compared to elementary schools, may provide fewer opportunities for self-selected peer interaction (Hirsch & DuBois, 1989). Access to peers as part of a social support network, in turn, may be important for students' adjustment to school.

The transition to middle school or junior high school can be particularly disruptive because the period of early adolescence, in which this transition is embedded, corresponds to the onset of puberty (Vondra & Gabarino, 1988). The onset of puberty typically corresponds to young adolescents' increased concerns with heterosexual relationships and appropriate gender role behavior (Furman, 1989). For example, more time is spent in opposite gender groups and less time in same gender groups across the adolescent period (Csikszentmihalyi & Larsen, 1984; Furman, 1989). Correspondingly, young adolescents must address changing gender-related roles for interacting with same- and opposite-gender peers. Because of the dual stresses associated with the onset of puberty and the transition to a new school setting, early adolescence has been identified as a period during which young people may be vulnerable to subsequent adjustment problems, such as antisocial behavior and neurosis, as well as more traditional academic problems (Sroufe & Rutter, 1984). Despite the recognized importance of this period for subsequent adjustment, very little is known about the ways in which young adolescents adjust to or fail to adjust to this transitional point. Further, there have been few longitudinal studies of students entering and progressing through middle school.

Different solutions have been proposed to "buffer" students' transitions from primary to secondary schools. Indeed, the middle school was created as an alternative to the junior high school, in hopes that the former would be a place where this transition could be eased, though there is no empirical support for this position (Entwisle, 1990). To conduct the research discussed in the present chapter, I chose a middle school as my research site. The extent to which this middle school was different from a junior high school or other middle schools was not part of the investigation. Indeed, this site was chosen because it was one of the few middle schools in the area that had an outdoor break period for students in the course of the school day.

Children's social networks, and the support they derive from them, have been proffered as a way in which some children adjust to new and stressful situations (see Belle, 1989, and Epstein & Karweit, 1983, for collections of papers on this issue). Social networks and social support can be defined along numerous structural dimensions, such as different roles represented in a network, for example, teachers, parents, grandparents, and peers; number of people in each role; and the frequency and extent of the contact (Tietjen, 1989). Networks also vary according to content dimensions, such as esteem support, informational support, instrumental support, and companion support (Bernt, 1989; Tietjen, 1989). These dimensions of social networks are typically assessed through questionnaire and/or interview methodologies. For example, Bernt and colleagues (Bernt, 1989; Bernt, Hawkins, & Hoyle, 1986), utilizing a longitudinal design, documented the changes in an aspect of social networks, friendships, from primary through the first year of junior high school and the ways in which aspects of friendships related to school adjustment.

In this chapter social networks are defined in terms of the number of different companions students had access to during their free time at school recess and the frequency with which they were nominated by their peers as being "liked most." As such, these networks were more akin to school social networks. Correspondingly, indexes of young adolescents' popularity were taken. The nature of these social relationships was addressed in terms of the behaviors that were exhibited in these groupings during their recess periods.

Access to different companions was defined as individuals being embedded in social groups, such as interacting with members of the same- and opposite-gender and the size of the peer groups in which these interactions take place. This definition of social embeddedness, or access to peers, lends itself very well to direct observational methodology. While inferences about the quality of the support cannot be made from direct observations, direct observations can be used to determine the extent to which boys and girls have access to peers, the composition of those groups, and the behaviors they exhibit in diverse groups.

Regarding access to peers and group composition, direct observation helps to answer a number of important questions. For example, do young adolescents interact in large or small groups? Are the groups gender-integrated or gender-segregated? This is a particularly important aspect of social networks because access to peers is an important indicator of one way in which social networks provide support. As I already noted, transition to a new school is difficult because it disrupts, or severs, students' social relationships. Adjustment to a new secondary school is probably a result of the ability to establish new relationships in the new school, rather than relying on network support from the previous school (Bernt, 1989). Consequently, access to various peer configurations during recess period in a new school is an important way in which students establish and re-enforce peer relationships.

Such a free period is one of the few times during the school day that students have free access to a variety of peers. While students may have access to peers in other contexts, such as in their neighborhoods or during extracurricular activities, play time is a scheduled part of the school day for students to interact among themselves. Consequently, this period is worthy of study.

The first objective of the study reported here was to examine the ways in which boys' and girls' social networks varied as they moved through the first two years of middle school. The importance of studying young adolescents as they progress through a new school environment, compared to studying their change from one school to another, is highlighted by Bernt's (1989) findings that friendship patterns within a new school, not the friendship patterns from the old school, were the important sources of social support. Results from extant interview and questionnaire research lead to specific hypotheses regarding students' companions.

First, gender differences in group size should be observed. It is well documented that boys have more extensive networks than girls (e.g., Feiring & Lewis, 1988; Waldrop & Halverson, 1975); thus, I expected boys' groups to be larger and more diverse than girls' groups. Gender differences should also be observed for composition of groups. "Sex cleavage" is a well-documented phenomenon where children from preschool through primary school (Belle, 1989; Feiring & Lewis, 1988; Hartup, 1983) interact more frequently in same-gender groups than in mixed-gender groups. As students move through middle school and become more interested in heterosexual relationships, I expected children to interact more in gender-integrated groups.

Correspondingly, early adolescents' interest in heterosexual relationships and mixed-gender groupings should relate to the types of behavior that are exhibited in these groups. Younger, compared to older, boys should exhibit more male stereotyped behavior, such as rough physical behavior (Pellegrini, 1992). This form of behavior should be limited to male predominant groups. When boys choose to interact with girls, however, boys should exhibit social sedentary behaviors, not rough behaviors. Similarly, girls should engage in social sedentary, not rough, behavior.

The extent to which children are "liked" and "not liked" by their peers is another way to measure children's social networks. Children receiving a large number of "likes most" nominations from peers have access to a larger network of peers than children with fewer "likes most" and more "likes least" nominations. The "widening circle" (Bernt, 1989) of popularity hypothesis states that as popular children progress through middle school their network of "likes most" nominations should provide a basis for a larger network. This grade effect may be moderated by gender to the extent that boys, more than girls, have more peers whom they "like most."

As I noted above, school social network variables should relate to young adolescents' adjustment to school. Because the transition to middle school is disruptive to students' accessibility to familiar peers, their access to peers at recess should provide particularly good insight into school adjustment. Different levels of access to social network variables should, in turn, relate differently to students' adjustment to middle school.

Adjustment to school, following Zigler and Trickett's (1978) notion of social competence, has achievement and social emotional components. In order to function in middle school students must achieve in subject matter and be socially and emotionally adjusted.

Achievement was measured by a composite measure of reading/mathematics. Social emotional adjustment was conceptualized in terms of two common components of psychopathology: students' antisocial behavior and neurosis (Rutter, 1967). Additionally, adjustment was conceptualized in terms of adolescents' sociometric status; being liked by peers is a positive indicator of adjustment while being rejected is a "worse case scenario" (Vondra & Garabino, 1988) of adjustment (Parker & Asher, 1987).

The extant literature examining the relation between social networks and intermediate school adjustment, with few exceptions, has been cross-sectional. Despite the gap in the literature, a number of hypotheses can be generated. First, with regard to children's achievement, the data are particularly spotty but there is interesting theory from the primate and ethological literatures (Humphrey, 1976; Jolly, 1966) suggesting that the size and diversity of one's social groupings should be positively related to cognitive status; the idea is that manipulating social others in the service of acquiring resources facilitates cognition. Extrapolating from these data, the extent to which adolescents are popular should relate to achievement as well.

Popularity and rejection are other important aspects of school adjustment. As I noted above, popularity with peers is an important indicator of adjustment because students who are not liked are typically "at-risk" on a number of counts, such as juvenile delinquency and dropping out of school (Parker & Asher, 1987). Aggression, and other forms of antisocial behavior, are reliable predictors of not being liked by peers. Further, young adolescents who are popular at the beginning of their intermediate school experience may use their friends to widen their supportive network (Bernt, 1989). Being liked by peers in early adolescence is often related to physical attractiveness (Lerner et al., 1991), skill in sports and games (Fine, Mortimer, & Roberts, 1990), and having access to large groups of peers (Bernt, 1989; Brown, 1990). These relations, however, may be different for boys and girls: the literature for elementary school children suggests that the routes to popularity and rejection are different for boys and girls (Asher & Coie, 1990).

The last aspects of school adjustment to be examined are common components of children's psychopathology: antisocial and neurotic personalities (Rutter, 1967). These two constructs are often differentially associated with gender to the extent that boys, more often than girls, exhibit externalizing disorders, such as antisocial behavior, while girls, more than boys, exhibit, internalizing disorders, like neurosis (Rutter & Garmezy, 1983). Antisocial personality may be related to the size of the groups that children choose to interact in to the extent that larger groups, compared to smaller groups, are more likely to have incidents of aggression that can be imitated (Maccoby, 1986). Additionally, being disliked by peers is associated with anti-social personality (Parker & Asher, 1987). The stability of aggression and antisocial personality across childhood and adolescence (Olweus, 1977, 1979), however, suggests that the relations among network variables, behavior, and antisocial personality should be intercor-related.

Neurotic personality, on the other hand, should be negatively related to group size, for neurotic youngsters withdraw rather than interact in groups. Further, because of the increased stress on het-erosexual relationships during adolescence, children's physical attractiveness should be negatively related to neurosis.

To sum up, there were two objectives to the research discussed in the present chapter: to examine the longitudinal change in male and female social networks across the first two years of middle school; and to determine the extent to which the social network, and other related measures, in the first year of middle school predicted adjustment to middle school in the second year.

Method

Subjects

The site of the study was a rural middle school, grades 6-8, in the southeastern United States. Students entering the school in the sixth grade were studied until the end of their seventh grade year, a two-year period. The sample was composed of 56 students (26 males and 30 females). Because the school is 97 percent Caucasian, only Caucasians were included in the sample to avoid a racial confound.

Procedures

From September of year 1 to June of year 2, a total of 22 months, students were observed on their school playground during their recess period. They were free to go outdoors during recess or to stay indoors. Approximately 75 to 150 students were in the outdoor space at any one time. The same two persons were observers for the duration of the study. Neither observer, however, was aware of stu-dents' status on any of the other measures collected on the student they observed.

Observations followed focal subject sampling and continuous recording rules (Martin & Bateson, 1986). Focal students were observed, in counterbalanced order, for 3 minutes. Their behavior was continuously recorded by having observers talking into portable tape recorders for 3 full minutes or until the focal child was out of sight. Observers stayed close enough so that they could record students' language and describe their facial expressions. In addition to recording behavior, the names, number, and gender of members of the focal student's immediate group was recorded. Data used in the study reported here was taken from students who were observed at least 10 times each for the two years. Thus, all subjects were observed as focal subjects at least 20 times.

The exhaustive and mutually exclusive system of playground behavior was based on the earlier work of Humphreys and Smith (1987). Here, only two behavioral categories will be analyzed: *rough behavior* and *social sedentary behavior*. Rough behavior included the following: play face, run with/without ball, stand with ball, watch the rough behavior, throw/catch ball, block/is blocked, tackle/ is tackled, play fight. Social sedentary behavior included the following: sit, stand, lie down, eat, talk with adult, talk with peer (away from rough), comfort contact/hug, groom, dress. Additionally, the number of peers in the immediate group and their gender was recorded, as was the duration (in 5-second intervals) of their outdoor stay. Additionally, *male peers*, *female peers*, and *group size*, were coded, as was *duration outdoors*. The peer and group measures were expressed in relative frequencies while the duration was expressed in seconds.

Reliability checks on the accuracy of the verbal encoding of the behavior information were made on 25 percent of the focal samples for each of the two years on the rough and passive categories. The *kappa* were .87 and .89, respectively.

Measures

A series of measures were administered to both students and their teachers each of the two years of the study. Administration was supervised by the two teachers who served as observers. As I noted above, the observers were blind to the status on the measures of the students they observed. The following measures were employed in the study.

"Likes most" and "likes least" was assessed by having individual students view pictures of the members of their homeroom, name them all, and then nominate three students they "liked most" and three they "liked least." The unit of analysis was the average number

of "likes most" and "likes least" nominations received by each student.

Homeroom teachers completed a battery of instruments on each child in the late autumn/early winter of each year. The battery was made up of the following instruments.

Coie and Dodge's Teacher Checklist (n.d.) has 45 items, each scored from 1 (low) to 5 (high). Four items were included in the data for present study: *physical attractiveness, ability at games,* and a collapsed *achievement score* for reading and math achievement levels (corresponding to F through A, respectively).

The Children's Behavior Questionnaire was developed by Rutter (1967) and consists of 26 items on which each child is rated 0 (doesn't apply), 1 (sometimes), or 2 (certainly applies). The questionnaire, which has been empirically verified by Rutter (1967), yields two factor scores: *Antisocial* and *Neurotic*.

Results

Social Network Analyses

The first series of analyses addressed the variation in children's social network variables as a function of gender and grade (sixth and seventh, from year 1 to year 2). Separate measures of children's social network included: number of "likes most" nominations, number of "likes least" nominations, number of boys interacted with on the playground, number of girls interacted with on the playground, group size on the playground, and the duration of children's stay on the playground. The descriptive statistics for these measures are displayed in Table 9.1.

A series of repeated measures ANOVA were calculated with grade (2: 6 and 7) as the within subjects factor and gender (2) as the between-subjects factor. All post hoc comparisons followed the Newman-Keuls procedure with a .05 *alpha*. Regarding the average number of "likes least" nominations received by individual children, a significant grade effect, $F(1,20) = 8.06, p < .01$, was observed, with sixth graders having more "likes least" nominations than seventh graders. For the average number of "likes most" nominations received by individual children, no significant variation was observed.

The next series of social network analyses were based on behavioral observations. The number of boys with whom the focal children interacted with was analyzed. During year 1 a significant gen-

TABLE 9.1

Descriptive Statistics for School Peer Network Measures

| | 6th | | 7th | |
	Boys	Girls	Boys	Girls
Liked least				
M	1.36	1.54	.56	.90
SD	.67	.87	1.12	1.37
Liked most				
M	1.84	2.44	1.15	2.33
SD	1.34	1.15	.83	1.61
Boy interactants				
M	2.53	.86	8.84	5.33
SD	3.20	2.43	18.69	16.88
Girl interactants				
M	.15	2.06	2.19	11.36
SD	.78	3.41	8.63	27.92
Group size				
M	.54	2.00	1.94	2.33
SD	.76	6.09	.56	1.18

der effect, F (1,55) = 4.91, $p < .03$, was observed, with boys, more than girls, interacting with boys, and so too was a significant grade effect, F (1,55) = 5.46, $p < .02$, with all seventh graders interacting with boys more often than sixth graders. Regarding girls as interactants, a significant gender effect, F (1, 55) = 7.79, $p < .007$, was observed for sixth graders, with girls, more than boys, interacting with other girls. A main effect for grade was also observed, F (1,55) = 3.93, $p < .05$, with seventh graders, more than sixth graders, interacting with girls. For group size, no significant grade or gender effects were detected.

Regarding duration on playground, during sixth grade a significant gender effect was observed, F (1,55) = 37.67, $p < .001$, with boys staying out longer than girls, and a significant gender × grade interaction, F (1,55) = 9.00, $p < .004$, with sixth and seventh grade boys staying out longer than sixth grade girls.

Teachers' Ratings of Neurotic and Antisocial Personalities

Separate gender × grade repeated measures analyses were conducted on each of the two factors from the Children's Behavior Questionnaire (Rutter, 1967). For the neurotic factor, no significant main or interactive effects were observed. For the antisocial factor, a significant main effect for gender was observed across the two years, F (1,48) = 3.97, p < .05, with boys (M = .74) being rated as more antisocial than girls (M = .20)

Contemporaneous Correlations between Network Variables and School Adjustment

In light of the gender × grade effects reported above, correlations will be reported separately, by grade and gender. Further, only significant correlations will be presented in text; all correlation coefficients are, however, displayed in the appropriate tables.

Sixth graders. For sixth grade boys, size of interaction group at recess was negatively correlated with achievement and positively correlated with social sedentary behavior, "likes most" nominations, and antisocial ratings. Facility with games was positively related to physical attractiveness and achievement and negatively related to neurotic and antisocial ratings and "likes least" nominations. Boys as interaction partners was positively correlated with social sedentary behavior and antisocial ratings but negatively correlated with physical attractiveness. Physical attractiveness was positively related to achievement and antisocial ratings. Duration on the playground was positively related to both social sedentary behaviors and rough behaviors. Relatedly, rough behavior was negatively related to "likes most" nominations. Neurotic ratings were positively related to antisocial personality and number of "likes most" nominations, while antisocial ratings were positively related to "likes least" nominations. Lastly, "likes least" nominations were negatively correlated with "likes most" nominations. These relations are displayed in Table 9.2.

Sixth grade girls' group size was positively related to interacting with both boys and girls, duration on the playground, and social sedentary behavior. Facility with games was negatively related to neurotic and antisocial ratings and "likes least" nominations. Interacting with boys was positively related to duration on playground and social sedentary behavior but negatively related to "likes most" nominations. Interacting with other girls was also positively related to duration and sedentary behavior. Physical attractiveness and achievement were both negatively related to "likes least" nominations. Duration outdoors was positively related to sedentary social behavior. Social sedentary behavior was, in turn, negatively related to antisocial ratings. The antisocial ratings were negatively related

TABLE 9.2

Intercorrelations for 6th Grade Boys

	2	3	4	5	6	7	8	9	10	11	12	13
Group size (1)	.12	.79***	-.10	-.30	-.33*	.15	.49***	-.05	.04	.33*	-.10	.35*
Games (2)		.11	-.27	.67=**	.50***	.09	.29	.22	-.37*	-.36*	-.35*	-.03
Boys int. (3)			.22	-.34*	-.32	.31	.74***	.24	.01	.43**	.12	.03
Girls int. (4)				.18	.09	.08	.06	.12	.23	-.10	.00	.00
Attract (5)					.54***	.03	.05	.15	-.17	.45**	-.28	-.13
Achieve (6)						.21	-.27	.06	.17	-.15	.38**	-.17
Duration (7)							.48**	.53***	-.24	.25	.01	.01
Soc. sed (8)								.46**	-.30	.23	.18	.21
Rough (9)									-.17	.12	.26	-.70***
Neur (10)										.34*	.78***	.28
Antisoc (11)											.63***	.00
Likes least (12)												-.40**
Likes most (13)												

*p < .10   **p < .05   ***p < .01

to "likes most" nominations while the neurotic ratings were positively related to "likes least" nominations and negatively related to "likes most" nominations. These relations are displayed in Table 9.3.

   Seventh graders. Seventh grade boys' (from year 2) duration outdoors was positively correlated with group size, and boy *and* girl interactants. Group size was negatively related to achievement rating, but positively related to games, male and female interactants, duration outdoors, neurotic personality rating, and "likes most" nominations. Boys' interactions with other boys was positively related to interacting with girls, duration outdoors, and sedentary social behavior, while their interactions with girls was positively correlated with duration outdoors. Physical attractiveness was negatively related to rough behavior and neurotic ratings but positively related to "likes most" nominations. Achievement was negatively related to "likes most" nominations and positively related to antisocial ratings. Duration outdoors was positively related to both sedentary social behaviors and rough behaviors. Rough behaviors and social sedentary behaviors were also positively intercorrelated. Neurotic ratings were positively related to antisocial ratings and "likes least" nominations and negatively related to "likes most" nominations. "Likes least" and "likes most" nominations were negatively intercorrelated. These correlations are displayed in Table 9.4.

   Regarding seventh grade girls, their group size was positively related to male and female interactants, duration outdoors, and "likes most" nominations. Their facility with games was positively related to physical attractiveness and negatively related to neurotic ratings. Interaction with boys was correlated with having girls as interactants as well as achievement, duration outdoors, and social sedentary behavior. Interacting with other girls was also positively correlated with duration and social sedentary behavior, as well as "likes most" nominations. Physical attractiveness was negatively related to neurotic and antisocial ratings. Neurotic ratings were, in turn, positively correlated with achievement. Duration outdoors was positively related to social sedentary behavior and neurotic and antisocial ratings. Neurotic and antisocial ratings were positively intercorrelated. These relations are displayed in Table 9.5.

Longitudinal Correlations between
Network Variables and Social Competence

   The zero-order correlations coefficients between measures of social competence and social network variables are presented sepa-

TABLE 9.3

Intercorrelations for 6th Grade Girls

	2	3	4	5	6	7	8	9	10	11	12	13
Group size (1)	.07	.32*	.53***	.25	-.20	.30*	.37**	.00	-.04	.01	-.20	.18
Games (2)		-.10	.14	-.09	.02	.04	.06	.00	-.45**	-.33*	-.35**	.18
Boys int. (3)			.10	.21	-.16	.47**	.32*	.00	-.01	.01	.04	-.57**
Girls int. (4)				.14	.07	.54**	.53**	.00	-.12	-.19	-.21	.09
Attract (5)					-.08	.22	.21	.00	-.30*	.10	-.65***	.01
Achieve (6)						.02	-.18	.00	-.20	-.05	-.60**	.09
Duration (7)							.60***	.00	.04	-.21	-.07	-.20
Soc. sed (8)								.00	.10	-.30*	.22	-.41**
Rough (9)									.00	.00	.00	.00
Neur (10)										.12	.67***	-.39**
Antisoc (11)											-.18	-.39**
Likes least (12)												-.03
Likes most (13)												

*p < .10   **p < .05   ***p < .01

TABLE 9.4

Intercorrelations for 7th Grade Boys

	2	3	4	5	6	7	8	9	10	11	12	13
Group size (1)	.51***	.70**	.57***	-.07	-.38**	.58***	-.16	.13	.34*	-.16	.07	.37*
Games (2)		.08	.18	.23	.12	-.24	-.33**	-.23	-.43**	.09	-.29	.13
Boys int. (3)			.91***	.23	.03	.65***	.52***	.06	-.10	.04	-.15	.23
Girls int. (4)				.32	.08	.47**	.28	-.11	-.15	.05	-.13	.28
Attract (5)					-.19	-.18	.10	-.37*	-.41**	-.31	.01	-.39**
Achieve (6)						.13	.11	.00	.31	.38**	-.31	-.42**
Duration (7)							.69**	.58**	-.11	.03	-.27	.25
Soc. sed (8)								.46**	.02	.08	-.27	.04
Rough (9)									.01	-.16	-.12	-.19
Neur (10)										.41**	.42**	-.58***
Antisoc (11)											-.24	-.28
Likes least (12)												-.37*
Likes most (13)												

*$p < .10$ **$p < .05$ ***$p < .01$

TABLE 9.5

Intercorrelations for 7th Grade Girls

	2	3	4	5	6	7	8	9	10	11	12	13
Group size (1)	-.27	.83***	.80***	-.02	.29	.55**	.06	.00	-.06	.13	-.18	.48**
Games (2)		-.14	-.10	.58**	-.07	-.22	-.02	.00	-.48***	-.19	-.05	.24
Boys int. (3)			.63***	.02	.48***	.49***	.39**	.00	.18	.18	.12	.23
Girls int. (4)				.16	.04	.66***	.51***	.00	-.03	-.05	-.05	.47***
Attract (5)					-.18	-.11	.15	.00	-.57**	-.51**	.01	.12
Achieve (6)						.01	.19	.00	.43**	.09	-.15	-.04
Duration (7)							.68***	.00	.38**	.33*	-.19	.22
Soc. sed (8)								.00	.22	.08	.18	-.06
Rough (9)									.00	.00	.00	.00
Neur (10)										.41**	-.22	-.07
Antisoc (11)											.14	-.12
Likes least (12)												-.09
Likes most (13)												

*p < .10   **p < .05   ***p < .01

rately for boys and girls in Tables 9.6 and 9.7, respectively. These correlations are useful in determining the year-to-year stability of these measures for boys and girls. For boys the following measures were significantly intercorrelated from year 1 to year 2: group size, achievement rating, sedentary social behavior, neurotic rating, antisocial rating, and "likes most" ratings. Regarding girls' year-to-year stability, the following measures were significantly intercorrelated: group size, game rating, interacting with boys, physical attractiveness, neurotic rating, "likes least" nominations, and "likes most" nominations.

Next partial correlations were calculated between sixth grade measures and seventh grade measures, separately for boys and girls; these partial correlation coefficients are displayed in Table 9.8. The strategy with these analyses was to control, or partial-out, the sixth grade values for the corresponding seventh grade measures. For example, the partial correlations for the seventh grade criterion measure "likes most" nominations would control sixth grade "likes most" nominations.

First, the "likes least" nominations will be presented. For both boys and girls, group size in sixth grade was a negative predictor of being liked least in seventh grade. Further, for boys, interacting with other boys was a negative predictor, while attractiveness was a negative predictor. For girls, game rating was negatively related.

"Likes most" nominations in seventh grade for boys was negatively predicted by rough play, while for girls it was positively predicted by group size, physical attractiveness, and social sedentary interaction.

In the next series of analyses, seventh grader neurotic and antisocial personality ratings were the criterion variables. For boys' neurotic ratings, the following measures were positive predictors: interacting with other boys, interacting with girls, duration outdoors, and sedentary social behavior. For girls' the following sixth grade measures predicted seventh grade neurotic ratings: physical attractiveness (negatively) and achievement ratings. Regarding seventh grade antisocial ratings, boys' sixth grade games rating was a positive predictor and girls' physical attractiveness was a negative predictor.

Children's seventh grade achievement ratings were also predicted. Boys' sixth grade game rating was a negative predictor while for girls group size and interacting with boys were positive predictors.

TABLE 9.6

Intercorrelations for 6th to 7th Grade Boys

	1	2	3	4	5	6	7	8	9	10	11	12	13
Group size (1)	.36*	-.47**	-.01	-.14	.11	.13	.14	.31	.12	.24	-.02	.29	.20
Games (2)	.09	.26	-.22	-.21	-.02	-.49***	-.18	-.11	.07	-.27	.27	-.09	.23
Boys int. (3)	-.55***	-.41**	.11	.05	.02	.35*	.15	.43**	.16	.41**	.20	-.17	.01
Girls int. (4)	.00	-.39**	-.09	-.05	-.15	.06	-.12	.18	.08	.38**	-.10	.26	-.22
Attract (5)	.21	.11	-.31	-.32	.07	-.43**	-.23	-.27	.08	-.26	-.00	.09	.11
Achieve (6)	.21	-.01	-.18	-.19	-.32	.35*	.07	-.26	.21	-.07	.05	.16	.04
Duration (7)	-.37*	-.17	.12	.03	.17	.02	.07	.45**	.23	.28	.20	-.10	.09
Soc. sed (8)	-.04	-.31	.20	.11	-.20	.12	.27	.40**	.18	.26	.16	.02	-.06
Rough (9)	-.09	-.17	.17	.16	-.01	-.27	.21	.21	.26	.10	.02	.03	-.26
Neur (10)	-.24	-.13	-.10	-.14	-.13	.11	-.12	.11	.13	.34*	.01	.03	-.32
Antisoc (11)	-.25	-.13	.27	.17	-.16	.65***	.24	.33**	.07	.57***	.54**	-.13	-.33**
Likes least (12)	-.33*	-.72***	-.05	-.18	-.25	.22	.34*	.43**	.61***	.60***	.06	.16	-.08
Likes most (13)	.35**	.16	.15	.03	-.26	-.15	.04	-.10	-.28	-.01	.05	-.26	.33*

*$p < .10$ **$p < .05$ ***$p < .01$

TABLE 9.7

Intercorrelations for 6th to 7th Grade Girls

	1	2	3	4	5	6	7	8	9	10	11	12	13
Group size (1)	.58***	.36**	.47***	.12	.13	.27	.02	-.04	.00	.03	.06	-.20	.47***
Games (2)	.02	.50**	-.19	.00	.23	-.24	-.28	-.40**	.00	-.35*	-.09	-.13	.25
Boys int. (3)	.56***	-.10	.46***	.09	-.17	.43***	.00	-.06	.00	.15	.15	-.02	-.10
Girls int. (4)	-.35*	-.13	.36**	-.05	.03	.22	.01	.01	.00	-.14	-.05	.00	.40**
Attract (5)	.01	.35*	.09	-.03	.43**	.13	-.25	-.05	.00	-.46***	-.42**	.16	.14
Achieve (6)	-.49***	-.12	.24	-.18	-.09	.06	-.30*	-.25	.00	.28	-.28	-.04	.01
Duration (7)	.35*	.51**	-.11	-.16	.07	-.09	.13	.00	.00	-.14	-.12	-.00	.04
Soc. sed (8)	.01	.25	.13	.14	-.15	.12	.16	.16	.00	-.04	.22	-.18	.20
Rough (9)	.00	.00	.00	.00	.00	.00	.00	.00	.00	.00	.00	.00	.00
Neur (10)	-.03	-.22	.00	-.12	-.54***	.35**	.41**	.19	.00	.50**	.50**	.00	-.08
Antisoc (11)	.56***	-.11	.10	-.04	-.09	.28	-.10	-.18	.00	.00	.00	-.04	.03
Likes least (12)	-.09	-.43**	-.21	-.23	-.71	.22	.57**	.24	.00	.87***	.77***	.41***	-.27
Likes most (13)	.24	.55***	-.33*	-.01	.68***	-.85***	-.05	-.40**	.00	-.61***	-.65***	.20	.47***

*p < .10   **p < .05   ***p < .01

TABLE 9.8

Partial Correlations for Boys' and Girls' 6th Grade Measures Predicting 7th Grade Adjustment

| | 6th Grade | | | | 7th Grade | | | | | |
| | Likes Least | | Likes Most | | Neurotic | | Antisocial | | Achievement | |
	Boys	Girls	Boys	Girls	Boys	Girls	Boys	Girls	Boys	Girls
Group size	-.38**	-.40**	-.05	.30*	.25	.06	.25	.06	.02	.33*
Games	.07	-.39**	.26	.09	-.17	-.16	.59**	-.09	-.40**	-.24
Boys int.	-.49***	.18	-.10	.19	.43**	.13	-.03	.15	.28	.46***
Girls int.	.00	-.12	.00	.22	.33*	-.12	-.05	.05	.14	.00
Attract	-.49***	-.11	.25	.37**	-.22	-.36**	.32	-.43**	.30	.15
Achieve	-.09	.20	.27	-.05	-.14	.47**	.17	-.28	-.16	.27
Duration	.11	.08	-.00	.15	.40**	-.23	.08	-.13	-.04	.09
Soc sed	.22	.01	.18	.47**	-.16	.17	.04	.23	.12	.15
Rough	-.18	.00	-.44**	.01	.00	.15	.04	.00	.18	.00

*p < .10   **p < .05   ***p < .01

Discussion

My first objective was to describe the changes in young adolescents' social networks as they moved through the first two years of middle school. As I expected, networks changed as a function of both gender and grade. Sixth grade boys and girls chose same-gender students, rather than opposite-gender students, with whom to interact during their recess. This gender cleavage dissipated, however, as students progressed through middle school. All students, as they moved from sixth to seventh grade, interacted with *both* more boys *and* with more girls. Thus, while sixth graders interacted more frequently in gender-segregated groups, as seventh graders they interacted more frequently with both more boys and more girls.

It may be that this reliance on same-gender peer groups in sixth grade reflects young adolescents' choice of same-gender peers as friends, and these friends, in turn, provided the social support necessary for children to interact in integrated groups. As students moved through their second year of middle school their circle widened to include more boys and girls.

Children's interactions with peers of the opposite gender is particularly relevant to the early adolescent period as it corresponds to the onset of puberty and heterosexual relationships. In this light, the behaviors that boys and girls exhibited when they were in same- and opposite-gender groupings was examined. Girls' interactions with both boys and girls, in both sixth and seventh grades, was positively correlated with social sedentary interaction. Boys in both grades, on the other hand, when they interacted with other boys, exhibited rough behavior. In the seventh grade boys' rough behavior was negatively related to having girls as interactants. These correlations suggest that as boys and girls interact more frequently together, boys' exhibit less stereotyped male behavior and more behavior that is characteristic of heterosexual relationships. Future research should address the actual language that children use in these various social grouping so as to more accurately describe the nature of these relationships.

As the second objective of this study, the longitudinal relations between social network variables in sixth grade and adjustment in seventh grade were explored. First, it should be noted that most of the social network variables were intercorrelated for both boys and girls for each of the two year measures. The intercorrelation among social network variables replicates other work with adolescents suggesting that social support comes from many interrelated sources, such as access to diverse companions and friends (Bernt, 1989).

About one-half of the adjustment variables were significantly intercorrelated across the two years. Specifically, for both boys and girls the following were significantly intercorrelated from year 1 to year 2: size of the peer group, neurotic ratings, and "likes most" nominations. For boys, achievement, antisocial ratings, and social sedentary behavior were also correlated across the two grades, while girls' games and physical attractiveness ratings, interactions with boys, and "likes least" nominations were significant.

It may be the case that measures of adjustment, like social network measures, are intercorrelated and stable because personality variables, like antisocial and neurotic personalities, are relatively stable and, in turn, determine other aspects of adjustment and social networks. Take, for example, the case of antisocial ratings. Aggression and antisocial behavior, as I noted above, are stable across this period (Olweus, 1977, 1979). Aggression, in turn, relates to children's rejected sociometric status (Coie, 1990), and size of the group with whom children interact (Ladd, 1983).

That about 50 percent of the adjustment variables were not significantly intercorrelated from year 1 to year 2 supports the notion that the first two years of middle school also represent a time of discontinuity for some children. The ways in which young adolescents adjust, or fail to adjust, to this change varies. To begin with what Vondra and Garbarino (1988) termed the worst case scenario, being rejected (i.e., liked least) by one's peers in seventh grade for both boys and girls is negatively predicted (determined by partial correlation coefficients) by the size of the interaction group in sixth grade. The present data show that boys' and girls' "liked least nominations" had different predictors. Based on the correlational evidence presented above, boys were probably liked least because they were antisocial and exhibited rough behavior. Antisocial behavior is a common basis for peer rejection (Asher & Coie, 1990; Coie, 1990). That group size was a negative predictor of "likes least" nominations is consistent with the idea that other youngsters, including other boys, do not interact frequently with rejected youngsters (e.g., Ladd, 1983). Girls, on the other hand, were disliked if their teachers rated them good at games. It may be that these girls were rejected by their peers because they violated sex-role stereotypes. The stereotype is that boys, not girls, should be good at games.

Next children's "likes most" nominations from their peers are considered. Boys' rough behavior negatively predicted their popularity, while for girls' sedentary social behavior, physical attractiveness, and size of peer group were significant predictors. Adolescent boys exhibiting rough behavior, unlike younger boys (Pellegrini, 1988), seem to do so to exhibit dominance and aggressive behavior; it tends not to be playful (Pellegrini, 1994). Consequently, it is not surprising that this form of agonistic behavior was a negative predictor of "likes most" nominations. This topic will be addressed specifically in the next chapter.

Boys' and girls' physical attractiveness was, respectively, a negative predictor of "likes least" and a positive predictor of "likes most" nominations. That physical attractiveness is important for sociometric status is well documented, particularly during this period of increased heterosexual relationships (Lerner et al., 1991). Additionally, girls are liked when they engage in passive social behavior in larger groups. It may be the case that girls's physical attractiveness in sixth grade provides an entree into larger seventh grade social groups, which are also gender-integrated. For girls, sedentary social interaction in these groups is a reliable predictor of being liked by one's peers.

Regarding seventh graders' neurotic personality ratings, girls' sixth grade achievement and physical attractiveness were positive and negative predictors, respectively. The transition to adolescence seems to put stress of girls and their developing gender roles in terms of physical attractiveness and academic achievement. These correlations are consistent with the data showing that adolescent girls, so as to conform to a specific gender stereotype, may suppress their exhibition of achievement-related behavior in school (Huston, 1983, pp. 409-410) and engage in abnormal eating/dieting practices, such as anorexia nervosa, because of their concern with physical attractiveness (Rutter & Garmezy, 1983, p. 868). Boys' neurotic personality ratings also can be explained in terms of violation of gender-stereotyped behavior. Boys' ratings were predicted by three inter-correlated behavioral measures: duration, interaction with boys, and interaction with girls. It was the case that boys, more than girls, chose to stay outdoors for longer periods. But sixth grade boys who interact frequently with girls are probably violating sex-role stereotypes. In seventh grade, when mixed-gender groupings are more common, this may not be a problem, but in sixth grade, where gender segregation is modal, it is atypical for boys to interact with girls. That some boys do so, even at a younger age (e.g., Ladd, 1983), may be an indicator of social emotional problems.

The antisocial ratings of boys in seventh grade were significantly predicted by their sixth grade facility in games, while for girls it was negatively predicted by physical attractiveness. The results for the boys can be explained by the fact that being good at games for adolescent boys often means team sports, like football and basketball (Fine et al., 1990). These activities are often aggressive and more often have boys, compared to girls, as participants; correspondingly, and as the data in the present study indicate, boys are typically rated by their teachers as more antisocial than girls. Thus, teachers typically consider boys and the activities that they engage in as anti-social, and often counter to the goals of school.

In summary, the present study revealed both continuity and discontinuity during the first two years of middle school. Certain personality, and corresponding behavioral, measures were stable across the two years. Further, the social networks of boys and girls differed substantially from each other and from sixth to seven grades. Networks became more gender-integrated across the period. Sixth grade social network measures, in turn, were predictors of seventh grade adjustment. Adjustment for boys and girls can be most parsimoniously explained in terms of children's learning and exhibiting gender-stereotyped behavior.

Finally, it should be noted that different types of measures predicted boys' and girls' maladjustment to school (i.e., "likes least" nominations and antisocial and neurotic ratings). Specifically, for girls, teachers' ratings accounted for three of the four significant partial correlations, whereas for boys, teachers ratings accounted for only two of six—behavioral measures accounted for the other four. This finding is in line with Kupersmidt and Patterson's (1991) work with preadolescent boys and girls. This issue is certainly worthy of future empirical examination.

References

Asher, S., & Coie, J. (Eds.). (1990). *Peer rejection in childhood.* New York: Cambridge University Press.

Belle, D. (1989). Gender differences in children's networks and supports. In D. Belle (ed.), *Children's social networks and social supports* (pp. 173-190). New York: Wiley.

Bernt, T. (1989). Obtaining support from friends during childhood and adolescence. In D. Belle (ed.), *Children's social networks and social supports* (pp. 308-331). New York: Wiley.

Bernt, T., Hawkins, J., & Hoyle, S. (1986). Changes in friendship during a school year. *Child Developmenmt, 57,* 1284-1297.

Brown, B. (1990). Peer groups and peer cultures. In S. Feldman & G. Elliot (eds.), *At the threshold* (pp. 171-196). New York: Cambridge University Press.

Coie, J. (1990). Toward a theory of peer rejection. In S. Asher & J. Coie (eds.), *Peer rejection in childhood* (pp. 365-402). New York: Cambridge University Press.

Csikszentmihalyi, M., & Larsen, R. (1984). *Being adolescent.* New York: Basic Books.

Davies, B. (1982). *Life in the classroom and playground.* London: Routledge.

Entwisle, D. (1990). School and the adolescent. In S. Feldman & G. Elliot (eds.), *At the threshold* (pp. 197-224). New York: Cambridge University Press.

Epstein, J., & Karweit, N. (Eds.). (1983). *Friends in school.* New York: Academic Press.

Feiring, C., & Lewis, M. (1988). The child's social network from three to six years. In S. Salzinger, J. Antrobus, & M. Hammer (eds.), *The social networks of children, adolescents, and college students* (pp. 93-112). Hillsdale, NJ: Erlbuam.

Fine, G., Mortimer, J., & Roberts, D. (1990). Leisure, work, and mass media. In S. Feldman & G. Elliot (eds.), *At the threshold* (pp. 225-252). Cambridge, MA: Harvard University Press.

Furman, W. (1989). The development of children's social networks. In D. Belle (ed.), *Children's social networks and social support* (pp. 151-172). New York: Wiley.

Hartup, W. (1983). Peer relations. In E. Hetherington (ed.), *Handbook of child psychology* (Vol. 4, pp. 103-196). New York: Wiley.

Hirsch, B., & DuBois, D. (1989). The school-nonschool ecology of early adolescence. In D. Belle (ed.), *Children's social networks and social support* (pp. 260-276). New York: Wiley.

Humphrey, N. (1976). The social function of intellect. In P. Bateson & R. Hinde (eds.), *Growing points in ethology* (pp. 303-317). Cambridge: Cambridge University Press.

Humphreys, A., & Smith, P. K. (1987). Rough-and-tumble play, friendship, and dominance in school children. *Child Development, 58,* 201-212.

Huston, A. (1983). Sex-typing. In E. Hetherington (ed.), *Handbook of child psychology* (Vol 4, pp. 387-468). New York: Wiley.

Jolly, A. (1966). Lemur social behavior and primate intelligence. *Science, 153,* 501-506.

Ladd, G. (1983). Social networks of popular, average, and rejected children in school settings. *Merrill-Palmer Quarterly, 29*, 283-308.

Lerner, R., Lerner, J., Hess, L., Schwab, J., Jovanovic, J., Talwar, R., & Kucher, J. (1991). Physical attractiveness and phychosocial functioning among early adolescents. *Journal of Early Adolescence, 11*, 300-320.

Maccoby, E. (1986). Social groupings in childhood. In D. Olweus, J. Block, & M. Radke-Yarrow (eds.), *The development of antisocial and prosocial behavior* (pp. 263-284). New York: Academic Press.

Martin, P., & Bateson, P. (1986). *Measuring behaviour*. London: Cambridge University Press.

Olweus, D. (1977). Aggression and peer acceptance in adolescent boys. *Child Development, 48*, 1301-1313.

———. (1979). Stability of aggressive reaction patterns in males. *Psychological Bulletin, 86*, 852-875.

Parker, J., & Asher, S. (1987). Peer relations and later personal adjustment. *Psychologocal Bulletin, 102*, 357-389.

Pellegrini, A. D. (1988). Elementary school children's rough-and-tumble play and social competence. *Developmental Psychology, 24*, 802-806.

———. (1992). Preference for outdoor play during early adolescence. *Journal of Adolescence, 15*, 241-254.

———. (1992b). Kindergarten children's social cognitive status as a predictor of first grade success. *Early Childhood Research Quarterly, 17*, 565-577.

———. (1994). The rough play of adolescents of differing sociometric status. *International Journal of Behavioural Development*.

Rutter, M. (1967). A children's behaviour questionnaire for completion by teachers. *Journal of Child Psychology and Psychiatry, 8*, 1-11.

Rutter, M., & Garmezy, N. (1983). Developmental psychopathology. In E. Hetherington (ed.), *Handbook of child psychology* (Vol 4, pp. 775-911). New York: Wiley.

Sroufe, S. A., & Rutter, M. (1984). The domain of developmental psychopathology. *Child Development, 55*, 17-29.

Tietjen, A. M. (1989). The ecology of children's social support networks. In D. Belle (ed.), *Children's social networks and social support* (pp. 37-69). New York: Wiley.

Vondra, J., & Garbarino, J. (1988). Social influences on adolescent behavior problems. In S. Salzinger, J. Antrobus, & M. Hammer (eds.), *Social networks of children, adolescents, and college students* (pp. 195-224). Hillsdale, NJ: Erlbaum.

Waldrop, M., & Halverson, C. (1975). Intensive and extensive peer behavior. *Child Development, 46,* 19-26.

Zigler, E., & Trickett, P. (1978). I.Q., social competence, and evaluation of early childhood intervention programs. *American Psychologist, 33,* 789-798.

10

Adolescent Boys' Rough-and-Tumble Play

Introduction

Rough-and-tumble play (R&T) has been described as a playful and affiliative category of social behavior that includes vigorous behaviors such as chasing and play fighting. This body of work consistently has shown that for preschool and elementary school children R&T is a male-preferred behavior (e.g., Humphreys & Smith, 1984) and a category, generally, distinct from aggression (Pellegrini, 1989a).

Regarding gender differences, the empirical record is quite clear. Males, more than females, engage in R&T (DiPietro, 1981; Maccoby & Jacklin, 1974; Pellegrini, 1989a). This robust difference has been observed in most nonhuman primate species (Smith, 1982) as well as cross-culturally among human children (Whiting & Edwards, 1973). Moreover, R&T seems to be positively related to aspects of social competence for most boys, but not for girls, from the preschool through the elementary school period (e.g., Pellegrini, 1989a).

The relation between boys' R&T and social competence and aggression, however, is not clear-cut. As I noted in Chapter 7, relations seem to vary as a function of boys' sociometric status. The R&T of popular, not rejected, elementary school children relates positively to measures of social competence, like engagement in cooperative games, while the R&T of rejected children often results in aggression (Pellegrini, 1988, 1989b). It seems that popular and rejected boys may be using R&T to serve different functions. Consequently, in this chapter the R&T of adolescent boys of different sociometric status groupings will be examined. Besides examining the R&T of popular and rejected boys, I will also examine a group of average boys to provide a comparison for these two extreme groups (Coie, Dodge, & Coppotelli, 1982).

Importantly, the role of R&T may change as boys move from childhood into adolescence. The research presented in Chapter 7 suggests that R&T for popular and rejected children has different trajectories across the elementary school period. Specifically, I demonstrated that the R&T of popular, not rejected, children was correlated both contemporaneously and longitudinally with engagement in cooperative games. R&T may serve as a bridge for popular children from more idiosyncratic social play, like R&T, to play that is governed by a priori rules. Thus, we would expect the R&T of this group to decrease as they move into adolescence. The R&T of rejected children, on the other hand, was related to aggression during childhood and did not lead to cooperative games (see also Price & Dodge, 1989).

The R&T of rejected children should remain high across childhood and into adolescence, possibly because they lack the skills to engage in cooperative games. Further, their R&T should continue to be related to aggression in light of the fact that rejected boys continue to be aggressive across childhood and early adolescence (Coie et al., 1982; Olweus, 1979). These relations, however, have, generally, not been explored beyond the period of childhood. As I discussed in Chapter 7, it seems that as boys move from childhood into adolescence the role of R&T changes. For older boys, R&T was negatively related to sociometric status (see Chapter 7) and positively related to some aspects of dominance (Humphreys & Smith, 1987).

Interesting theoretical questions arise with the study of R&T during early adolescence. Specifically, the animal play literature suggests that R&T serves a different function in early adolescence than it does during early childhood (Fagen, 1981; Symons, 1978). It has been suggested that while R&T is playful and prosocial during childhood, it may be more aggressive and related to dominance during early adolescence. Because dominance status is in a state of flux during early adolescence, "cheating" at R&T may be used as a way to maintain or establish dominance status (Fagen, 1981).

The "Cheating Hypothesis" of play, as advanced by Fagen (1981), proposes that children enter R&T bouts assuming they are playful. Cheating occurs when one party turns play into aggression or a dominance display so as to extract some benefit, like dominance exhibition, over an unsuspecting playmate. Cheating at R&T, according to this theory, is the mindful exploitation of a situation that involves being able to choose a playmate who can be exploited. Consistent with this reasoning Humphreys and Smith (1987) found that 11-year-olds, but not 7-year-olds, chose to initiate R&T with playmates of lower dominance status, suggesting that such choices were indicative of using R&T to serve a dominance exhibition function (Humphreys & Smith, 1987).

The Humphreys and Smith study was an important first step in this line of research but it was limited in important ways. First, children's gender and sociometric status were not differentiated and thus their study confounded age comparisons. R&T, as I noted above, seems to serve different functions according to children's gender and sociometric status; consequently, these variables must be separated. Second, they utilized a cross-sectional research design to study developmental changes in the relation between R&T and dominance.

To study development, generally, longitudinal designs are desirable (McCall, 1977). A longitudinal design is certainly necessary to determine the extent to which R&T in year 1 predicts dominance status in subsequent years. Additionally, more specific questions, such as the role of R&T for boys ascending and descending in dominance status as they enter adolescence, can only be addressed using a longitudinal research design.

To address this dominance exhibition issue it is also important to break down R&T into two components: chase (R&T/Chase) and physically rough play (R&T/Rough). While this distinction is typically made in the animal literature and by some child ethologists (e.g., Harlow & Harlow, 1965; Smith & Boulton, 1990; Symons, 1974, 1978), it is rarely made by child developmentalists. The distinction is an important one in that each set of behaviors has distinctive motor patterns and seems to serve different functions (Symons, 1978). Chasing should be more beneficial in terms of physical fitness, whereas rough play should provide opportunities to practice skills useful in dominance exhibition and fighting (Smith, 1982; Smith & Boulton, 1990). Consequently, one would not expect the chase dimension of R&T, which includes running after and away from peers, to be related to dominance or aggression because little rough, physical contact is involved. Further, as I illustrated in Chapter 9, chase is a relatively immature behavior. To the extent that the vigorous movement are not embedded in games, one would expect adolescents to engage in low-level R&T/Chase. Rough play, like play fighting, on the other hand, represents an excellent opportunity to exploit the usually playful tenor of R&T. Children can be easily exploited when they put themselves in a subordinate play fight position, such as by being pinned. Further, any injury inflicted might be dismissed as an "accident," or to use Fagen's (1981) term, an "honest mistake." The honest mistake interpretation can be dismissed in favor of the cheating interpretation, however, when the following criteria are met: boys systematically choose less dominant playmates for this rougher form of R&T, and R&T/Rough is correlated with aggression and dominance and leads to aggression.

Following this logic, one would expect rejected boys to use R&T/Rough as a way in which to exploit playful interaction for their own dominance exhibition ends. Their use of R&T/Rough for aggressive ends as adolescents would be a continuation of a similar pattern described during childhood. Popular boys, on the other hand, should exhibit R&T/Rough at lower rates than other groups of boys. Regarding the R&T/Rough of average boys, one would predict initial similarity to rejected boys in that they both, during childhood, engage in R&T and physical aggression at similar rates; these rates are greater than those for popular boys (Coie & Kupersmidt, 1982). With age, average boys may not resemble the rejected group to the extent that boys, generally, are less concerned with physical prowess and more concerned with social support as a way to maintain status among peers (Coie & Kupersmidt, 1983).

As the first objective of the research presented in this chapter, the age- and sociometric status-related changes in both types of R&T and aggression will be presented. As the second objective, the relations between both forms of R&T and dominance will be examined. This will be accomplished in two ways. First, the relation between boys' R&T/Chase and R&T/Rough and their peers nominated dominance status will be determined. This will be done within each of the two years and between years. Significant relations between R&T/Chase and dominance are not expected for the reasons stated above. Regarding R&T/Rough, however, a correlation with dominance is expected for rejected and average boys because of the research showing that they engage in R&T and aggression at similar rates (Coie & Kupersmidt, 1983). It is my contention that R&T is being used by these boys for dominance exhibition. Popular boys, on the other hand, do not usually engage in behaviors that exhibit dominance physically, such as aggression (Coie & Kupersmidt, 1982; Pellegrini, 1991b).

The second way in which the relation between R&T and dominance will be examined is by describing playmate choice. This too will be done within each of the two years and from year 1 to year 2. Within year, following Humphreys and Smith (1987) and the procedures I outlined in Chapter 7, focal boys' dominance status will be compared with the status of their playmates for each of the two types of R&T. Unlike previous research, however, this will be done for boys of different sociometric status and for two dimensions of R&T. It is expected that average and rejected boys will initiate R&T/Rough with children of lower dominance status (Pellegrini, 1991a). Such asymmetry should not be observed in R&T/Chase because it is not a category that lend itself to physical domination.

The longitudinal relations between R&T and dominance will also be studied in terms of boys who are increasing and decreasing in peer-nominated dominance status from year 1 to 2. Specifically, I, following Fagen, expect that boys moving up in dominance status should choose R&T partners of *both* higher and lower dominance status, while those descending in status should choose mates of lower status. The confidence of boys ascending in dominance allows them to use all opportunities to exhibit dominance. For boys whose dominance status is decreasing, partners of lower status should be chosen. In this way they attempt to maintain their higher status. It is expected that boys who are declining in dominance status from year 1 to year 2 should pick R&T/Rough playmates of lower dominance status in an attempt to maintain their high status.

My third objective in the study whose results are presented in this chapter was to further examine boys' cheating at R&T/Rough. Cheating can be inferred through "motivational analyses," or the extent to which individual R&T/Rough bouts lead to aggression at lag 1. If children consistently turn R&T into aggression, we can assume they are cheating. Data from these sequential analyses, as well as correlation data between R&T and dominance and R&T and aggression, and playmate choice data, will be used to test the cheating hypothesis.

Method

Subjects

The site of this study was the same as that discussed in Chapters 8 and 9. In brief, it was a rural middle school in the southeastern United States. Sixth and seventh grade homerooms (N = 138 and 167, respectively) were recruited for the research. The average age of the boys was 13.25 years at the beginning of year 1 of the study. Only Caucasian boys were included in the study so that ethnicity did not confound the sample.

The sociometric status of all boys was determined according to procedures outlined by Coie et al. (1982). In the late fall of each year, individual children sat in front of an array of pictures of their classmates and were first asked to name all the children. Next, they were asked to name three children they liked the least and three they liked the most. Following Dodge, Coie, Petitt, and Price (1990), the number of "liked most" and "liked least" nominations were added and standardized into social preference and social impact scores. Popular children were those with a social preference Z-score greater than .8; rejected children were those with social preference scores of less than −.8; average children were those with social preference and social impact scores between +.8 and −.8. Following Dodge and colleagues (1990), the .8 criterion was used to maximize sample size. This procedure resulted in the identification of 22 popular boys, 19 average boys, and 13 rejected boys. The year 1 to year 2 correlation for social preference was $r = .46$, $p < .0005$, and for social impact was $r = .58$, $p < .0001$.

Procedures

From September in year 1 to June in year 2, a total of 22 months, children were observed during their recess periods in the school playground, composed of a courtyard and walkways. The grassy part of courtyard area was of rectangular shape and measured approximately 25 × 35 meters; asphalt walkways and other grassy surface bordered the courtyard. Approximately 75 to 150 children were in the courtyard at any one time.

The same two persons were observers for the full duration of the study. Neither, however, was aware of children's sociometric or dominance status. Children were observed according to focal child sampling and continuous recording rules (Martin & Bateson, 1988). Focal children were observed, in counterbalanced order, for 3 minutes. Their behavior was recorded continuously for 3 minutes or until they were out of sight for 30 seconds. Observers stayed close enough to focal children so that they could see their facial expressions and hear their language. Observers recorded the focal child's name, behavior, the children with whom the focal child was interacting, the number of children in the immediate group, and the location on the playground; all this was done by talking into small tape recorders. The continuous recording maintained the sequential integrity of the data. Data presented here are taken from children who were observed a minimum of 10 times per year across the two-year period.

The exhaustive and mutually exclusive category system of children's playground behavior used in this report was based on earlier work of Humphreys and Smith (1987) and Pellegrini (1988). Only

R&T and aggression dimensions will be described here. In differentiating R&T from aggression a list of default rules was followed such
that raters judged affect (play face vs. frown); reciprocity versus uni-
laterality; and separation versus affiliation. In cases of ambiguity, all
three criteria were applied. In other, more clear-cut cases, all three
criteria were not needed; for example, in a fight in which children
were unwilling to separate, the separation criterion was not needed
for the classification.

R&T/Chase: play face, run after/from another, tag/tagged, jump,
    tug/tugged at. Children stay together after the initiation of
    R&T/Chase.
R&T/Rough: play face, run with/without ball, stand with ball,
    watch while in R&T/Rough group, throw/catch ball, block/is
    blocked, tackled/tackles, playfight. Children stay together after
    the initiation of R&T/Rough.
Aggression: fixate/frown, hit with closed hand or kick (where contact
    is made), and grab and push. One child tries to leave after the
    initiation of aggression.

For these measures, only bouts initiated by focal children were
included. The unit of analysis for the behavioral data was the relative frequency with which the individual bouts of the behaviors of
interest were observed; the frequency of the target behaviors were
divided by the total behaviors observed. A bout was defined as con-
tiguous behaviors belonging to the same superordinate category, for
example, blocked then tackled would be aggregated under one
R&T/Rough bout. When a behavior from outside that category was
observed, for example, hit with closed hand, a new bout was scored.

Reliability checks were made at two levels. First, the accuracy
of the verbal encoding of the focal child's behavior into the tape
recorder was determined for each of the two years. This was accomplished by having two observers simultaneously encoding the behavior of the same focal child. Comparisons of the observers were made
in terms of the behaviors encoded (at the subordinate levels within
R&T/Rough, R&T/Chase, and aggression and other behaviors not
included in this study) and the names and number of participants
involved on 25 percent of the tapes for each of the two years; the
level of agreement was .85 (*kappa*). The second level of reliability
involved checking the accuracy with which the verbal encodings
were assigned to the superordinate behavioral categories. This was
accomplished by a third person, not involved in the observations,

who recoded 25 percent of the tapes; the level of agreement was .92 across the two years.

Children's dominance status was assessed in each of the two years, following Humphreys and Smith (1987) and as outlined in Chapter 7, by having them rank-order the children in their class-rooms. More specifically, as part of the sociometric interview, children were asked to identify, in order, the toughest children in their class. Children received a mean rank-order score reflecting the mean of the ranks across their classmates. Scores were transposed such that higher scores represented higher dominance status. This approach to having children rate dominance status, compared to using behavioral measures of dominance, has been shown to be highly reliable for early adolescents (Boulton & Smith, 1990; Savin-Williams, 1979). Because children tend to overrate their own dominance status, their ratings of themselves were not included. The dominance status of boys in the three sociometric groups was compared with a one-way analysis of variance (ANOVA) and a significant effect was observed., F (1,51) = 14.73, p < .0004; rejected boys were most dominant; average boys were more dominant than popular boys.

Results

The first objective of this study was to describe the changes in boys' R&T and aggression as a function of sociometric status and age. Both dimensions of R&T and aggression were analyzed in terms of relative frequency of occurrence. Sociometric status was a between-subjects variable at three levels and age was a within-subjects variable at two levels. Data were analyzed in separate repeated measures analyses of variance (ANOVA). Post hoc comparisons were made using the Students'/Newman-Keuls procedure with a .05 *alpha*. The descriptive statistics for aggression and R&T are displayed in Table 10.1.

First, regarding aggression, there was no significant variation for sociometric group, F (2,53) = .73, p < .48, age, F (1,53) = .12, p < .12, or group × age, F (2,53) = .76, p < .76. Similarly, for R&T/Chase, no significant variation was observed for group, F (2,53) = .39, p < .71, age, F (1,53) = .36, p < .55, or group × age, F (2,53) = .62, p < .54. For R&T/Rough, significant main effects for group, F (2,53) = 3.72, p < .03, and age, F (1,53) = 10.93, p < .001, were observed, as well as a significant group × age interaction, F (2,53) = 4.50, p < .01. Regarding the main effect for group, the rejected and average boys

TABLE 10.1

Descriptive Statistics for Aggression and R&T
by Year and Sociometric Status

	Average		Popular		Rejected	
	M	SD	M	SD	M	SD
Aggress						
Yr 1	.07	.32	.00	.00	.09	.36
Yr 2	.25	.83	.40	1.30	.27	.95
R&T/Ch						
Yr 1	3.41	4.91	4.46	1.76	2.08	3.74
Yr 2	4.65	6.81	3.19	4.59	4.80	9.29
R&T/R						
Yr 1	24.46	25.47	5.31	6.69	15.06	26.08
Yr 2	3.91	9.51	3.56	9.56	8.96	17.83

exhibited similar levels of R&T/Rough; both were significantly higher
than the R&T/Rough of popular boys. Further, significantly more
R&T/Rough was observed in year 1 than in year 2. The age × group
interaction, which mediated these main effects, suggests that within
year 1 the average and rejected boys engaged in R&T/Rough at similar levels and they were both greater than the popular boys. At
year 2, however, the rejected boys engaged in significantly more
R&T/Rough than both average and popular boys, whereas the latter
two groups were similar.

Next, the relation between the two forms of R&T and dominance was examined for boys in the three sociometric groups. This
was done at two levels: calculating correlation coefficients between
each form of R&T and dominance and by examining boys' R&T playmate choice. The correlation are displayed in Table 10.2. Generally,
R&T/Chase was not significantly related to dominance in either
year. R&T/Rough, on the other hand, was significantly related to
dominance for boys in all three groups during year 1 and for the
average and rejected boys in year 2. The correlations between
R&T/Rough in year 1 and dominance in year 2 indicated that
R&T/Rough in year 1 was positively and significantly related to dominance in year 2 for rejected, $r = .64$, $p < .05$, and average boys, $r =
.46$, $p < .05$. When partial correlations were calculated between year
1 R&T/Rough and year 2 dominance, controlling year 1 dominance,
only the correlation for rejected boys remained significant, $rp = .58$,
$p < .05$.

TABLE 10.2

Intercorrelations among R&T, Aggression, and Dominance by Year

Year	Dominance (1)			Aggression (2)			R&T/Chase (3)			R&T/Rough (4)		
	1	2	1-2	1	2	1-2	1	2	1-2	1	2	1-2
Average (n = 19)												
1			.69**	.49**	.21	.27	.53***	.19	.21	.58***	.43*	.33
2			.23			.07	.06	.08	.17	.29	.06	.10
3			.39*			.35			.03	.18	.07	.08
4			.46**			.08			.52***			.42*
Popular (n = 22)												
1			.70***	.00	.20	.18	.13	.1	.17	.38**	.28	.45**
2			.00			.00	.00			.00	.30	.03
3			.12			.20			.17	.05	.36	.39*
4			.25			.05			.10			.32
Rejected (n = 13)												
1			.62**	.21	.34	.30	.02	.11	.09	.82***	.69**	.54*
2			.36*				.17	.16	.12	.54*	.62**	
3			.14			.17			.18	.006	.23	.04
4			.64***			.16			.07			.51

*p < .10   **p < .05   ***p < .01

Next, comparisons of playmate choice in R&T/Chase and R&T/Rough was made for boys in each of the three groups. Comparisons were first made within years 1 and 2. Next, longitudinal comparisons were made by separately comparing playmate choice for boys increasing and decreasing in dominance status. Comparisons were made by making pair-wise comparisons in dominance status between the focal boys and each of their playmates in R&T/Chase and R&T/Rough bouts. Only bouts initiated by the focal boys were analyzed. The extent to which the ratings of the focal boys and their playmates differed from chance was calculated by the sign test. Specifically, this was accomplished by comparing the rank of the focal boy with the rank of each participant, individually, in each bout. Within year 1, the R&T/Chase analyses indicated that average and popular boys played with others of *higher* dominance status at a greater than chance level, $p < .01$. For the year 1 R&T/Rough category, rejected and average boys played with others of *lower* dominance status at a greater than chance level, $p < .05$. The year 2 data suggest that R&T/Chase playmate choice did not differ from chance for any group. For R&T/Rough during year 2, however, rejected boys chose others of *lower* dominance status at a greater than chance level, $p < .05$, while popular boys chose others of *higher* status at a greater than chance level, $p < .01$.

For the longitudinal analysis of playmate choice the following procedure was followed. Boys were put into one of two groups: those ascending in rank from year 1 to year 2 (.8 of a standard deviation above the mean for those increasing in dominance) and those descending in rank (.8 of a standard deviation below the mean for those decreasing in dominance). Next, the extent to which boys in each of the two groups chose to play with others of higher or lower status was examined. The extent to which these pairings were greater than chance was determined using similar procedures as used for the within-year playmate analyses. Boys ascending in dominance engaged in R&T/Rough in year 2 with others of both higher and lower dominance status. Boys descending in dominance status, on the other hand, chose to engage in R&T/Rough with boys of *lower* status at a greater than chance level, $p < .05$. Additionally, for the R&T/Rough bouts that turned into aggression within year 2, 83 percent were initiated by boys who were ascending in dominance status from year 1 to 2.

The last series of analyses examined the relation between R&T and aggression. The relevant correlations are displayed in Table 10.2. R&T/Chase was not related to aggression in either year, while

R&T/Rough was significantly correlated with aggression for rejected boys in both year 1 and in year 2. At a more proximal level, sequential lag analyses revealed that individual R&T/Rough bouts of rejected boys led to aggression at a greater than chance level, $z = 2.79$, during year 1 only.

Discussion

The first objective of the research reported here was to describe the effects of age and sociometric status on boys' R&T/Chase, R&T/Rough, and aggression. There was no significant variation in either the R&T/Chase or aggression categories. R&T/Chase is a relatively "immature" behavior for young adolescents. At the beginning of adolescence boys have the cognitive capability to engage in games with rules (Piaget, 1965). Where adolescent boys want to engage in a physically vigorous activity, like chase, they are more likely to choose a rule-governed activity, like sports (Coie & Whidby, 1986; also see Chapters 8 and 9). That R&T/Chase did not vary by sociometric status is also consistent with work by Boulton (1989) with a sample of English middle school children.

Similarly, aggression did not vary significantly by age or sociometric status. This may be a result of the generally low rates of aggression observed, though these rates are similar to those reported in other studies where aggression was observed on elementary and middle school playgrounds (Humphreys & Smith, 1987; Pellegrini, 1989a). School policy that explicitly prohibits aggression is probably responsible for the low rates of aggression generally observed.

R&T/Rough, however, did vary significantly by age and sociometric status. The extent to which boys engaged in this form of vigorous rough play declined significantly from year 1 to year 2. This decline may have been due to a number of factors. First, cross-sectional research indicates that R&T declines during this period (Humphreys & Smith, 1984). Second, a life span developmental perspective (Entwisile, 1990) suggests that such developmental changes interact with the institutions in which children are embedded. As boys move through adolescence and middle school their interests turn from gender-segregated, physically vigorous activities, like R&T/Rough, to less vigorous and less-gender-segregated activities, such as pursuing heterosexual relationships (Entwisile, 1990; Pellegrini, 1992). Future research might address these issues by studying children who are moving from childhood to adolescence but attending different types of school, in which there are different stresses on heterosexual relationships, such as 12-year-olds in a middle school compared to an elementary school for grade 6.

A third explanation for the decrement in R&T/Rough is that children, with time, became less willing to engage in an activity in which they could be exploited and the only children left with whom to engage in R&T/Rough are "victims," or children who are prone to being bullied (e.g., Perry, Kusel, & Perry, 1986). Future research should address this issue directly.

The fourth, and preferred explanation, is that boys used R&T/Rough at higher levels in year 1 than in year 2 as a method to establish dominance. After dominance relationships were established there was probably less need to exhibit these behaviors in year 2. The specific ways in which dominance and R&T/Rough were related will be discussed below.

Regarding the effect of sociometric status on R&T, popular boys engaged in R&T/Rough at low rates throughout the two year duration of the study. They may have avoided R&T/Rough because of its relation to aggression and their aversion to aggression.

The younger average and rejected boys engaged in R&T/Rough with a similar frequency but with age the rejected boys engaged in more R&T/Rough than the average boys. This difference may be due to the fact that the rejected, not average, boys continued to use R&T/Rough as a venue from which they could be aggressive. The significant correlation between R&T/Rough and aggression for rejected boys supports this interpretation. That R&T/Rough was significantly correlated with aggression for rejected boys, even though there were low rates of aggression, suggests this is a robust relation. Rejected adolescents, like younger rejected boys (Pellegrini, 1988), also used R&T/Rough for their own aggressive ends. Consequently, the use of R&T for this group remained constant from childhood to early adolescence.

The second objective of this study was to examine the relations between R&T and dominance. It was hypothesized, based on the nonhuman primate play literature (Fagen, 1981; Symons, 1978), that R&T is used by adolescents to serve a dominance exhibition function. Unlike the R&T of preadolescents, which is generally cooperative and prosocial, evidence exists that early adolescents may actually cheat at play so as to exploit their playmates. In this study only the R&T/Rough, not the R&T/Chase, category was correlated with dominance and aggression. During the first year of the study R&T/Rough and dominance was significantly intercorrelated for boys in all sociometric groups; for the second year they were significantly intercorrelated for average and rejected boys. Further, during year 1 both average and rejected boys also chose to engage in R&T/Rough with others of lower dominance status; this pattern of partner choice was continued by the rejected boys in year 2. Though R&T/Rough and dominance were significantly intercorrelated for popular boys during year 1, it was probably not used to establish or reinforce dominance relationships; it did not meet other criteria for supporting the cheating hypothesis, that is, correlation with and direct antecedent to aggression, prediction of dominance, and occurrence with playmates of lower status. Consequently, the R&T of popular adolescents, like that of younger children (Pellegrini, 1988), does not seem to serve a dominance or aggressive function. On the other hand, the R&T/Rough of average and rejected boys, at least during year 1, seemed to serve a dominance function.

The playmate choice data presented here replicate and extend previous research showing that younger children engage in R&T in symmetrical groups; during early adolescence they play in asymmetrical groups (Humphreys & Smith, 1984). The present data extend this line of research by explicating the distinctive patterns of partner choice for different types of R&T for boys of differing sociometric status across a two-year span. R&T/Rough seems to be used by average and rejected adolescent boys to exhibit dominance. This was done by choosing an R&T/Rough playmate of lower dominance status. That their R&T/Rough was significantly correlated with dominance each year indicates that R&T/Rough was implicated in dominance, but not by immediate escalation into aggression or by predicting dominance from year 1 to year 2. Future research should address the specific behavioral strategies used by this group to establish and reinforce dominance. It may be the case that this group chose weaker boys to play with, not to aggress against them but to manipulate them in other ways, such as being less reciprocal in their play.

For rejected boys, on the other hand, when year 1 dominance was controlled, year 1 R&T/Rough was still a significant predictor of year 2 dominance; thus, the R&T/Rough of rejected boys was used to establish a dominance function from year 1 to year 2. That rejected boys cheated at R&T/Rough for dominance exhibition is most convincingly demonstrated by their turning R&T/Rough bouts into aggression, at a beyond chance level, during year 1. That R&T/Rough turned into aggression at a statistically significant rate during year 1, but not during year 2, may be due to the fact that these boys had already established themselves as dominant and cheaters at

R&T/Rough during year 1. Just as the need to fight to exhibit dominance decreases as dominance status is established, so too the need
to turn R&T into aggression may diminish. Rejected boys still
engaged in R&T/Rough and aggression during year 2 but at lower
contingency levels. These lower levels may reflect rejected boys' use
of R&T/Rough to reinforce the previously established relationship.

The similarity in R&T/Rough between the rejected and average
boys in the first year of the study merits discussion. Extant literature
suggests that average and rejected preadolescent boys (in familiar
groups) are similar in terms of their levels of rough play and fighting
(Coie et al., 1982); thus, one might expect initial between-group
resemblance. The change in year 2 between the rejected and the
average groups in the present study was probably due to the average
boys' assimilating into the culture of middle school where such rough
behavior is less common and where dominance moves from an
aggressive base to a more affiliative base (Zabriski & Wright, 1991).
In year 2 the R&T/Rough of average and popular boys was similar,
while that of the rejected boys remained high. In this way both average and popular boys were similar.

These results, like other research with younger children
(Pellegrini, 1988) suggest that the R&T of rejected, but not popular, elementary school boys is related to aggression. Thus, there is
continuity from childhood through adolescence in the relation
between R&T and aggression for rejected boys. That the R&T of
other, less extreme, adolescent children is related to aggression and
dominance is consistent with Neill (1976), who also found that R&T
of adolescent boys co-occurred with aggression. This pattern in early
adolescence is different from that reported for younger children in
Chapter 7. Regarding playmate choice, Humphreys and Smith (1987)
found that 11-year-olds, but not 7-year-olds, chose R&T playmates of
lower dominance status. In short, adolescent boys seem to use
R&T/Rough to exhibit dominance and occasionally to be aggressive.
It may be that dominance exhibition and occasional aggression in the
context of R&T/Rough, but not in the context of R&T/Chase, is more
easily overlooked, and considered an "honest mistake," by teachers
and peers because it is a playful, but rough, context. The systematic
nature of the partner choice for this particular behavior leads me to
question the mistake interpretation and endorse the cheating interpretation.

The longitudinal data on partner choice further support this
claim. Boys systematically chose R&T/Rough partners so as to maximize their dominance status. Consistent with Fagen's (1981)

hypothesis, boys increasing in status chose for R&T/Rough partners others of both higher and lower status. It may that they wanted to take every opportunity they could to exhibit dominance. They seemed to have done so by turning R&T/Rough into aggression. Such a strategy seems extreme, and a high-risk venture, in light of the high costs (e.g., punishment and/or being injured) and the relatively low gains (e.g., exhibition of one victory in a context that could be interpreted by peers as play). Such extremism, however, is probably remembered by participants, even those of higher dominance. The higher status boys may be unwilling to further escalate the aggression level with such a determined opponent (Popp & DeVore, 1974, cited in Fagen, 1981), particularly in light of the fact that dominance during this period is moving from an aggressive to an affiliative basis (Zabriski & Wright, 1991).

It would be interesting to know the extent to which these "extreme" boys were also risk-takers in other aspects of their lives. Boys decreasing in status, on the other hand, chose partners of lower status. They too were concerned with dominance exhibition, but tried to choose partners they were sure of dominating. In short, they were trying to reinforce their dominance status. Future research on the role of R&T might be directed at children whose dominance status is in transition, rather than the R&T of boys of different sociometric status groups.

In conclusion, these results suggest that two forms of R&T serve seemingly different functions. Unlike previous research with younger children which suggested that R&T was a cooperative and playful activity (see Smith & Boulton, 1990, for a review), the present study showed that during early adolescence a rough variant of R&T was consistently correlated with dominance status. The choice of playmates, for rejected and average boys too, supports this interpretation. Indeed, it seems that some boys cheat at R&T by turning it into aggression.

These findings, however, could be extended in future research. First, a longer time span would have been beneficial in documenting changes in the role of R&T from childhood through adolescence. The present study relied on extant literature with younger children to document the role of R&T in social competence. In the present study, those results were used as a base line from which to compare the adolescent results. A second, and related, future research direction involves utilization of a larger sample size. These results should be replicated with a larger sample, even though they are congruent with theory and extant data.

References

Blurton Jones, N. (1972). Categories of child-child interaction. In N. Blurton Jones (ed), *Ethological studies of child behavior* (pp. 97-129). New York: Cambridge University Press.

———. (1976). Rough-and-tumble play among nursery school children. In J. Bruner, A. Jolly, & K. Sylva (eds.), *Play—Its role in development and evolution* (pp. 352-363). New York: Basic Books.

Boulton, M. (1989). *A multimethodological investigation of rough-and-tumble play, aggression, and social relationships in middle school children.* Unpublished Ph.D. thesis, Sheffield University, Sheffield, United Kingdom.

Boulton, M., & Smith, P. (1990). Affective bias in children's perceptions of dominance. *Child Development, 61,* 221-229.

Coie, J., Dodge, K., & Coppotelli, H. (1982). Dimensions and types of social status: A cross-age perspective. *Developmental Psychology, 18,* 557-570.

Coie, J., & Kupersmidt, J. (1983). A behavioral analysis of emerging social status in boys' groups. *Child Development, 54,* 1400-1416.

Coie, J., & Whidby, J. (1986, April). *Gender differences in the basis of social rejection in childhood.* Paper presented at the annual meeting of the American Education Research Association, San Francisco.

DiPietro, J. (1981). Rough-and-tumble play. A function of gender. *Developmental Psychology, 17,* 50-58.

Dodge, K., Coie, J., Petitt, G., & Price, J. (1990). Peer status and aggression in boys' groups: Developmental and conceptual analyses. *Child Development, 61,* 1289-1309.

Entwisile, D. (1990). School and the adolescent. In S. Feldman & G. Elliot (eds.), *At the threshold* (pp. 197-224). Cambridge, MA: Harvard University Press.

Fagen, R. (1981). *Animal play behavior.* New York: Oxford University Press.

Harlow, H., & Harlow, M. (1965). The affectional systems. *Behavior of nonhuman primates, 2,* 287-334.

Humphreys, A., & Smith, P. K. (1984). Rough-and-tumble play in preschool and playground. In P. K. Smith (ed.), *Play in animals and humans* (pp. 241-270). Oxford: Blackwell.

———. (1987). Rough-and-tumble play, friendship, and dominance in school children: Evidence for continuity and change with age. *Child Development, 58,* 201-212.

Ladd, G. (1983). Social networks of popular, average, and rejected children in school settings. *Merrill-Palmer Quarterly, 29,* 283-307.

Maccoby, E., & Jacklin, C. (1974). *The psychology of sex differences.* Stanford, CA: Stanford University Press.

Martin, P., & Bateson, P. (1986). *Measuring behavior.* London: Cambridge University Press.

McCall, R. (1977). Challenges to a science of developmental psychology. *Child Development, 48,* 333-344.

Neill, S. (1976). Aggressive and non-aggressive fighting in twelve-thirteen pre-adolescent boys. *Journal of Child Psychology and Psychiatry, 17,* 213-220.

Olweus, D. (1979). Stability and aggressive reaction patterns in males: A review. *Psychological Bulletin, 86,* 852-875.

Pellegrini, A. (1988). Rough-and-tumble play and social competence. *Developmental Psychology, 24,* 802-806.

———. (1989a). Elementary school children's rough-and-tumble play. *Early Childhood Research Quarterly, 4,* 245-260.

———. (1989b). What is a category? The case of rough-and-tumble play. *Ethology and Sociobiology, 10,* 331-341.

———. (1991a, September). *The rough-and-tumble play of adolescent boys of differing sociometric status.* Paper presented at the annual meetings of the British Psychological Society—Developmental Section, Cambridge, United Kingdom.

———. (1991b). A longitudinal study of popular and rejected children's rough-and-tumble play. *Early Education and Development, 2,* 205-213.

———. (1992). Preference for outdoor play during early adolescence. *Journal of Adolescence, 15,* 241-254.

Perry, D., Kusel, L., & Perry, L. (1986). Victims of peer aggression. *Developmental Psychology, 24,* 807-814.

Price, J., & Dodge, K. (1989). Reactive and proactive aggression in childhood: Relations to peer status. *Journal of Abnormal Child Psychology, 17,* 455-471.

Piaget, J. (1965). *The moral development of the child.* New York: Free Press.

Rubin, K., Fein, G., & Vandenberg, B. (1983). Play. In E. M. Hetherington (ed.), *Handbook of child psychology: Socialization, personality, and social development* (pp. 693-774). New York: Wiley.

Savin-Williams, R. (1979). Dominance hierarchies in groups of early adolescents. *Child Development, 52*, 142-151.

Smith, P. K. (1982). Does play matter? Functional and evolutionary aspects of animal and human play. *Behavioral and Brain Sciences, 5*, 139-184.

——— . (1989). The role of rough-and-tumble play in the development of social competence. In B. Schneider, J. Nadel, & R. Weissberg (eds.), *Social competence in developmental perspective* (pp. 239-255). Hingham, MA: Kluwer.

Smith, P. K., & Boulton, M. (1990). Rough-and-tumble play, aggression, and dominance. *Human Development, 33*, 271-281.

Smith, P. K., & Connolly, K. (1972). Patterns of play and social interaction in preschool children. In N. Blurton Jones (ed.), *Ethological studies of children's behavior* (pp. 65-95). New York: Cambridge University Press.

Symons, D. (1974). Aggressive play and communication in rhesus monkeys (*Macaca mulatta*). *American Zoologist, 14*, 317-322.

——— . (1978). *Play and aggression: A study of rhesus monkeys.* New York: Academic Press.

Whiting, B., & Edwards, C. (1973). A cross-cultural analysis of sex-differences in the behavior of children age 3 through 11. *Journal of Social Psychology, 91*, 171-188.

Zabriski, A., & Wright, J. (1991, April). *Perceptions of dominance in children's peer groups: Age differences in the relation between aggression, status, and dominance.* Poster presented at biennial meetings of the Society for Research in Child Development, Seattle.

11

Conclusions and Implications

The topic of this book was what children do on their school playground during the recess. As I have noted, probably *ad nauseam*, this is the time of day that children love. They love it, it seems, because it is one of the few times during the school day that they get a chance a chance to interact with their peers and do things on their own terms. In light of this truth, it is quite curious, to me at least, that recess has not been studied more extensively. After all, this is a time during which children are "actively" involved, to use a term that is as ubiquitous and understudied as recess. In this final chapter I will suggest that what we have learned about children at recess and their social cognitive development can be useful in continued study of children's learning and development.

The Actively Engaged Child

Many students of early childhood education suggest that we as educators of young children should consider children as "active" learners. The "actively" engaged child is typically evoked as part of developmentally appropriate curricula, as well as other child-centered pedagogy. Activity is seen as an important component in motivation to learn. Interestingly, though, the "active" child remains elusive, in part due to poor definition. That is, active is not often explicated clearly: how do we know an active child when we see one?

The play literature provides some guidance here. Some definitions of play include the notion of the active child (e.g., Rubin, Fein, & Vandenberg, 1983). By "active," they mean that children have choice of an activity and once that activity is chosen they can define the nature of the interaction on their own terms. Of course, choice and definition exist within a set of parameters. For example, children may be able to choose among a set of activities and have a set of options while working on them.

The importance of these attributes in education have been recognized since at least Dewey's (1938) time. Providing children with opportunities to make choices and to define task meaning and solutions are important both for motivation and for lifelong learning. Again, following Dewey's pragmatism, children learn and develop by doing and interacting. Further, these are attributes that young adults are expected to exhibit in the work force (Heath, 1989). The modern workplace is based on the premise that workers will make a series of decisions in concert with fellow workers. So, the extent to which school provides these opportunities probably relates directly to the effectiveness of their training workers for the twenty-first century.

That recess allows children to make choices about who to interact with and who to avoid, as well as to socially negotiate the subsequent interaction, seems important in this light. Indeed, that children's social behaviors with peers on the playground relates to and predicts their social competence may have little to do with recess per se. It is probably the case that those interaction components that come under the rubric "active child" and "reciprocal interaction" happen to occur at recess. If we had classrooms where more peer interaction was permitted, we would probably find that these peer interaction variables within the classroom would also predict social competence. In preschools, where such interaction is normative, this seems to the case (Pellegrini, 1984; Wright, 1980). In short, I suggest that we should consider the social context when we consider children in schools.

The Social Context of School

While concern for children in the social context of school is certainly not novel, especially in light of the current stress on Vygotskian theory, I think we should study more systematically the specific aspects of social context and the ways in which they relate to learning and cognitive development. For example, what are the cognitive consequences of children interacting with more-or-less familiar peers? On the one hand, research indicates that interacting with someone with whom children are less familiar facilitates children's language development (Bernstein, 1960; Pellegrini, Galda, & Rubin, 1984). In theory, in situations in which participants share minimal knowledge and context they must verbally explicate meaning: they cannot rely on shared knowledge assumptions. The use of these language forms is an important dimension of schooling, generally (e.g.,

Cook-Gumperz, 1979), and of school-based literacy, specifically (e.g., Olson, 1977).

On the other hand, when children interact with familiar peers, especially friends, a number of important things happen that do not usually happen among less familiar participants or nonfriend acquaintances. For example, participants who meet repeatedly are more likely to cooperate than those who meet only a few times (Trivers, 1985). The idea here is that children will minimize antisocial behavior when there is a probability that they will be repaid in kind. This attention to the balance sheet of interaction, we know, fosters cooperation and altruism.

Cooperative interaction, in turn, will likely result in complementary interactions, characteristic of teaching, and reciprocal interactions, typical of play. Both of these interaction forms are important educational strategies. Again, we need to know more specifically about the outcomes of these different forms of interaction. While Piaget talked about the facilitate effects of peer interaction (because of its reciprocity), researchers have not, generally, attended to the ways in which these specific interaction forms relate to learning and development. Instead, researchers have been concerned with contrasts at grosser levels, such as those between peer interaction and adult interaction, with little concern for the relationships between the participants. We know, for example, that children and adults can and do engage in both reciprocal interaction *and* complementary interaction. When children and adults play, their interaction is reciprocal, yet in the teaching context, the interaction is complementary.

By way of guidance, Robert Hinde's (1980) model of relationship is a very useful heuristic for examining the specific interaction styles of the individual. Interaction is conceptualized as transactions among individuals' biology and social and physical environments. The following example illustrates the point using the friendship relationship. Children with a certain temperament may be more likely to become friends than other sorts of children. These children, when they are in friendship groups, compared to their being with a group of acquainted peers, will be more likely to cooperate, to disagree and then resolve the disagreement, and to take chances. So, for example, they may be more willing to try a problem-solving strategy which they are not exactly sure about with a group of friends, than with a less familiar group, because they can probably predict the groups' reaction. Thus, novel strategies and intellectual risk taking may be a by-product of children's relationship. Predictability, which is also characteristic of friendship dyads, in turn, may relate to metacognition. Specifically, by observing the consequences of specific actions in a group, children, and others, may be more likely to anticipate reactions. Such planned anticipation of actions and strategies, it seems to me, is an important instructional dimension.

Merely comparing children in peer groups, with those alone or with adults, would miss this point altogether: the relationship itself determines the interaction.In short, we as educators and child developmentalists need to study more thoroughly the social contexts in which children are embedded. The consequences of natural social groupings may provide important information for redesigning school. In this book, I have chosen one such context: recess. While we also have rich descriptions of mother-child and father-child contexts (Maccoby & Martin, 1983), as well as sibling contexts, it seems to me that we should now look into other contexts in both the school and the community and study the ways in which these context influence each other.

The Playground Recess Period as a Window into "Mind"

That children's social interaction with peers on the playground has social cognitive implications has been a recurrent theme in this volume. The above discussion was just another dimension. In this section I would like to talk specifically about a point raised in Chapter 6. Recall in that chapter I noted that what kindergarten children did on the playground at recess accounted for more variance in their first grade achievement scores than did a standardized measure of their kindergarten achievement.

While the low predictive validity of standardized test scores for young children is hardly news in the 1990s, what is news is that specific forms of social interaction, or what could be labeled "play," accounted for a significant portion of the variance in children's achievement. While theory for this connection has been around for years in various forms, such as Piaget's notion of the value of peer interaction, we are only beginning to design instructional and assessment contexts with similar levels of motivation for children.

My point is that play and other forms of activity, such as many of the behaviors that children exhibit on the playground, are powerful predictors of competence. There are at least two reasons for this. First, participation in many of these events are very demanding for most of these children. These high-demand situations elicit the highest levels of competence that children can muster. It is well documented that cooperative peer interaction requires a number of high-level cognitive strategies, such as conversational skills, perspective-taking, and rule compliance. Obviously, high cognitive demand is not enough.

The second component, motivation, is crucial. Children must want to perform at the high levels that are demanded by these tasks. Hence, the importance of play. Children are highly motivated to play simply because they enjoy it. Thus, they are willing to expend the cognitive resources necessary to participate in events they deem worthy of such effort. If you doubt the value of this observation, just compare the levels of oral language that preschoolers use when they are engaging in social fantasy play with the forms of oral language these same children use in assessment contexts. For an example involving adults, compare the effort that most college football players exhibit for football, a task they value, with the effort most expend on academics, a less valued task.

The implications of this for education are clear. We as educators should design instructional and assessment tasks that are motivating for children. Play is but one example. It might be the case that for school systems concerned with assessing kindergarten children, playground observations would be a good starting point.

References

Bernstein, B. (1960). Language and social class. *British Journal of Sociology*, 2, 217-276.

Cook-Gumperz, J. (1977). Situated instructions. In S. Ervin-Tripp & K. Mitchell-Kernan (eds.), *Child discourse*. New York: Academic Press.

Dewey, J. (1938). *Experience and education*. New York: Colliers.

Heath, S. B. (1989). Oral and literate traditions among black Americans living in poverty. *American Psychologist*, 44, 376-373.

Maccoby, E., & Martin, J. (1983). Socialization in the context of the family. In E. M. Hetherington (ed.), *Manual of child psychology* (Vol. 4, pp. 1-102). New York: Wiley.

Olson, D. (1977). From utterance to text. *Harvard Educational Review*, 47, 257-281.

Pellegrini, A. D. (1984). The effects of classroom play centers on preschoolers' functional uses of langauge. In A. D. Pellegrini & T. Yawkey (eds.), *The development of oral and written language in social context*. Norwood, NJ: Ablex.

Pellegrini, A. D., Galda, L., & Rubin, D. (1984). Context in text. *Child Development*, *55*, 1549-1555.

Rubin, K., Fein, G., & Vandenberg, B. (1983). Play. In E. M. Hetherington (ed.), *Handbook of child psychology* (Vol. 4). New York: Wiley.

Trivers, R. (1985). *Social evolution*. Menlo Park, CA: Benjamin-Cummings.

Wright, M. (1980). Measuring the social competence of preschool children. *Canadian Journal of Behavioural Science*, *12*, 17-32.